WORLD MOTORCYCLE GUIDE

Exeter Books

NEW YORK

in association with Phoebus

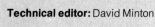

Technical editor: David Minton

While the publishers have made every effort to ensure that the information in this book is correct, they cannot be responsible for any alterations to technical specifications which have taken place since going to press.

This material first appeared in *1980 World Motorcycle Catalogue* © 1979 Edizioni A.I.D. SPA Milano © 1979 Phoebus Publishing Company/BPC Publishing Limited English Edition

First published in U.S.A. 1979 by Exeter Books Distributed by Bookthrift New York, New York

ISBN 0-89673-039-5 Library of Congress 79-91115

Made and printed in Great Britain by Purnell & Sons Ltd., Paulton (Bristol)

This year, as in each preceding year, more and more people are taking to the road on two wheels instead of four. Lately, this demand has been greatly increased by rapidly rising fuel costs and continuing shortages.

The choice facing the would-be bike buyer is, however, bewildering. But there is a machine available to suit almost every taste and requirement. This edition of the *World Motorcycle Guide* contains more than 160 bikes from the United States, Europe, Japan and the Soviet Union. Each one is illustrated in full colour and carries a complete technical specification.

We have reduced the number of mopeds from the last edition of the book, as well as featuring metric and imperial capacities. The entries include tourers, trials bikes and motocross fun bikes.

WORLD MOTORCYCLE GUIDE

KTM COMET 50

Engine: 49 cc single cylinder water-cooled two-stroke, maximum output 6.25 bhp (DIN) at 7,100 rpm. Bore and stroke 40×39.7 mm. Compression ratio 10:1. 19 mm Bing carburettor. 24:1 petroil lubrication. Kick start.
Transmission: primary drive by gears; final by chain. Five-speed gearbox. Wet multiplate clutch.
Ignition: Thyristor.
Frame: tubular cradle.
Suspension: front, telescopic forks; rear, swinging arm.
Tyres: front, 2.75×17; rear, 2.75×17.
Brakes: front, 245 mm disc; rear,

245 mm disc.
Tank capacity: 2.1 gallons (9.5 litres).
Weight: 203 lbs (92 kg).
Maximum speed: approximately 53 mph (85 km/h).

Manufacturer: KTM-Kronreif & Trunkenpolz, A 5230 Mattighofen.

KTM 125 MC

Engine: 124 cc single cylinder two-stroke, maximum output 26 bhp (DIN) at 9,500 rpm. Bore and stroke 54×54 mm. Compression ratio 11:1. 34 mm Bing carburettor. 24:1 petroil lubrication. Kick start.
Transmission: primary drive by gears; final by chain. Five-speed gearbox. Wet multiplate clutch.
Ignition: Motoplat contactless.
Frame: tubular duplex cradle.
Suspension: front, Ceriani telescopic forks; rear, swinging arm.
Tyres: front, 3.00×21; rear, 4.00×18.
Brakes: front, 130 mm drum; rear,

180 mm drum.
Tank capacity: 1.5 gallons (7 litres).
Weight: 209 lbs (95 kg).
Maximum speed: not stated.

Manufacturer: KTM-Kronreif & Trunkenpolz, A 5230 Mattighofen.

KTM 250 MC

Engine: 245 cc single cylinder two-stroke, maximum output 40 bhp (DIN) at 8,000 rpm. Bore and stroke 71×62 mm. Compression ratio 10:1. 36 mm Bing carburettor. 24:1 petroil lubrication. Kick start.
Transmission: primary drive by gears; final by chain. Six-speed gearbox. Wet multiplate clutch.
Ignition: Motoplat contactless.
Frame: tubular duplex cradle.
Suspension: front, telescopic forks; rear, swinging arm.
Tyres: front, 3.00×21; rear, 4.50×18.
Brakes: front, 130 mm drum; rear,

180 mm drum.
Tank capacity: 1.8 gallons (8 litres).
Weight: 214 lbs (97 kg).
Maximum speed: not stated.

Manufacturer: KTM-Kronreif & Trunkenpolz, A 5230 Mattighofen.

KTM 400 MC

Engine: 356 cc single cylinder two-stroke, maximum output 42 bhp (DIN) at 6,700 rpm. Bore and stroke 82×68 mm. Compression ratio 12:1. 38 mm Bing carburettor. 24:1 petroil lubrication. Kick start.
Transmission: primary drive by gears; final by chain. Six-speed gearbox. Wet multiplate clutch.
Ignition: Motoplat contactless.
Frame: tubular duplex cradle.
Suspension: front, telescopic forks; rear, swinging arm.
Tyres: front, 3.00×21; rear, 4.50×18.
Brakes: front, 130 mm drum; rear,

180 mm drum.
Tank capacity: 1.8 gallons (8 litres).
Weight: 218 lbs (99 kg).
Maximum speed: not stated.

Manufacturer: KTM-Kronreif & Trunkenpolz, A 5230 Mattighofen.

KTM 400/250 GS

Engine: 346 (245) cc single cylinder two-stroke, maximum output 44 (36) bhp (DIN) at 6,900 (7,400) rpm. Bore and stroke 80×69 (71×62) mm. Compression ratio 10:1. Bing 38 (36) mm carburettor. Petroil lubrication. Kick start.
Transmission: primary drive by gears; final by chain. Six-speed gearbox. Wet multiplate clutch.
Ignition: electronic.
Frame: tubular duplex cradle.
Suspension: front, telescopic fork; rear, swinging arm.
Tyres: front, 3.00×21; rear, 4.50×18.
Brakes: front, 130 mm drum; rear, 180 mm drum.
Tank capacity: 2.2 gallons (10 litres).
Weight: 227 (225) lbs (103 [102] kg).
Maximum speed: not stated.

Manufacturer: KTM–Kronreif & Trunkenpolz, A 5230 Mattighofen.

PUCH COBRA 6C 50/75

Engine: 49.9 (71.9) cc single cylinder two-stroke, maximum output 6.5 (10) bhp (DIN) at 8,500 rpm. Bore and stroke 40 (48)×39.7 mm. Compression ratio 11:1. 20 mm Dell'Orto carburettor. 24:1 petroil lubrication. Kick start.
Transmission: primary drive by gears; final by chain. Six-speed gearbox. Wet multiplate clutch.
Ignition: Motoplat Thyristor contactless. 6v.
Frame: duplex cradle.
Suspension: front, telescopic forks; rear, swinging arm.
Tyres: front, 2.50×20; rear,
3.25×18.
Brakes: front, 120 mm drum; rear, 110 mm drum.
Tank capacity: 1.5 gallons (7 litres).
Weight: 185 lbs (84 kg).
Maximum speed: approximately 50 (53) mph (80 [85] kmh).

Manufacturer: Steyr-Daimler-Puch AG, Puchwerke, Graz/Thondorf.

PUCH COBRA GTL

Engine: 49.9 cc single cylinder water-cooled two-stroke, maximum output 6.5 (10) bhp (DIN) at 8,500 rpm. Bore and stroke 40×39.7 mm. Compression ratio 11:1. 20 mm Bing carburettor. 24:1 petroil lubrication. Kick start.
Transmission: primary drive by gears; final by chain. Six-speed gearbox. Wet multiplate clutch.
Ignition: Bosch electronic. 6v.
Frame: duplex cradle.
Suspension: front, telescopic forks; rear, swinging arm.
Tyres: front, 2.50×17; rear, 3.00×17.
Brakes: front, disc; rear, drum.

Tank capacity: 2.8 gallons (12.5 litres).
Weight: 214 lbs (97 kg).
Maximum speed: approximately 56 mph (90 kmh).

Manufacturer: Steyr-Daimler-Puch AG, Puchwerke, Graz/Thondorf.

PUCH MONZA

Engine: 48.8 cc single cylinder two-stroke, maximum output 5.5 bhp (DIN) at 8,000 rpm. Bore and stroke 38×43 mm. Compression ratio 11:1. 17 mm Bing carburettor. 19:1 petroil lubrication. Kick start.
Transmission: primary drive by gears; final by chain. Four-speed gearbox. Wet multiplate clutch.
Ignition: Bosch flywheel magneto. 6v.
Frame: open cradle.
Suspension: front, telescopic forks; rear, swinging arm.
Tyres: front, 2.50×17; rear, 2.75×17.
Brakes: front, 140 mm disc; rear,

drum.
Tank capacity: 2.2 gallons (10 litres).
Weight: 163 lbs (74 kg).
Maximum speed: approximately 47 mph (75 kmh).

Manufacturer: Steyr-Daimler-Puch AG, Puchwerke, Graz/Thondorf.

PUCH GS 175 FRIGERIO

Engine: 173.6 cc single cylinder two-stroke, maximum output 30 bhp (DIN) at 8,500 rpm. Bore and stroke 62×57.5 mm. Compression ratio 13:1. Bing carburettor. Petroil lubrication. Kick start.
Transmission: primary drive by gears; final by chain. Six-speed gearbox. Wet multiplate clutch.
Ignition: electronic.
Frame: duplex cradle.
Suspension: front, telescopic forks; rear, swinging arm.
Tyres: front, 3.00×21; rear, 4.00×18.
Brakes: front, 135 mm disc; rear,

135 mm disc.
Tank capacity: 2 gallons (9.2 litres).
Weight: 205 lbs (93 kg).
Maximum speed: not stated.

Manufacturer: Steyr-Daimler-Puch 4G, Puchwerke, Graz/Thondorf.

PUCH MC 250 FRIGERIO

Engine: 247 cc single cylinder two-stroke, maximum output 38 bhp (DIN) at 8,500 rpm. Bore and stroke 74×57.5 mm. Compression ratio 13.5:1. 32 mm Bing carburettor. 24:1 petroil lubrication. Kick start.
Transmission: primary drive by gears; final by chain. Five-speed gearbox. Wet multiplate clutch.
Ignition: Bosch Thyristor contactless. 6v/35w.
Frame: tubular duplex cradle.
Suspension: front, telescopic forks; rear, swinging arm with gas shock absorbers.
Tyres: front, 3.50×21; rear,

4.50×18.
Brakes: front, 140 mm drum; rear, 160 mm drum.
Tank capacity: 1.7 gallons (7.5 litres).
Weight: 205 lbs (93 kg).
Maximum speed: not stated.

Manufacturer: Steyr-Daimler-Puch AG, Puchwerke, Graz/Thondorf.

PUCH GS 250 FRIGERIO

Engine: 247 cc single cylinder two-stroke, maximum output 36 bhp (DIN) at 8,500 rpm. Bore and stroke 74×57.5 mm. Compression ratio 12.5:1. 32 mm Bing carburettor. 24:1 petroil lubrication. Kick start.
Transmission: primary drive by gears; final by chain. Six-speed gearbox. Wet multiplate clutch.
Ignition: Bosch Thyristor contactless. 6v/35w.
Frame: tubular duplex cradle.
Suspension: front, telescopic forks; rear, swinging arm with gas shock absorbers.
Tyres: front, 3.50×21; rear,

4.50×18.
Brakes: front, 140 mm drum; rear, 160 mm drum.
Tank capacity: 2 gallons (9.2 litres).
Weight: 209 lbs (95 kg).
Maximum speed: not stated.

Manufacturer: Steyr-Daimler-Puch AG, Puchwerke, Graz/Thondorf.

CZ 250 DE LUXE

Engine: 246 cc two cylinder two-stroke, maximum output 18 bhp (DIN) at 5,250 rpm. Bore and stroke 58×58 mm. Compression ratio 9.3:1. 24 mm Jikov carburettor. 24:1 petroil lubrication. Kick start.
Transmission: primary drive by chain; final by fully-enclosed chain. Four-speed gearbox. Wet multiplate clutch.
Ignition: battery and coil. 6v/60w dynamo.
Frame: tubular cradle.
Suspension: front, telescopic forks; rear, swinging arm.
Tyres: front, 3.00× 18; rear, 3.25×18.
Brakes: front, 160 mm drum; rear, 160 mm drum.

Tank capacity: 2.9 gallons (13 litres).
Weight: 311 lbs (141 kg).
Maximum speed: approximately 75 mph (120 kmh).

Manufacturer: Ceskezavody Motocyklove NP, Strakonice.

JAWA 350

Engine: 343 cc two cylinder two-stroke, maximum output 23 bhp (DIN) at 5,250 rpm. Bore and stroke 58×65 mm. Compression ratio 9.2:1. 26 mm Jikov carburettor. Positive pump lubrication. Kick start.
Transmission: primary drive by chain; final by fully-enclosed chain. Four-speed gearbox. Wet multiplate clutch.
Ignition: battery and coil. 6v/75w dynamo.
Frame: tubular duplex cradle.
Suspension: front, telescopic forks; rear, swinging arm.
Tyres: front, 3.25× 18; rear, 3.50×18.
Brakes: front, 160 mm drum; rear, 160 mm drum.

Tank capacity: 3.6 gallons (16.2 litres).
Weight: 353 lbs (160 kg).
Maximum speed: approximately 78 mph (125 kmh).

Manufacturer: Jawa NP, Tynel Nad, Sazavou.

MZ TS 125/150

Engine: 123 (143) cc single cylinder two-stroke, maximum output 10 (11.5) bhp (DIN) at 6,000–6,300 rpm. Bore and stroke 52 (56)×58 mm. Compression ratio 10:1. Central float carburettor. 33:1 petroil lubrication. Kick start.
Transmission: primary drive by chain; final by fully-enclosed chain. Four-speed gearbox. Wet multiplate clutch.
Ignition: battery and coil ignition. 6v/40–45w dynamo.
Frame: pressed sheet steel.
Suspension: front, telescopic forks; rear, swinging arm with adjustable shock absorbers.

Tyres: front, 2.75×18; rear, 3.00×18.
Brakes: front, 160 mm drum; rear, 150 mm drum.
Tank capacity: 2.8 gallons (12.5 litres).
Weight: 227 lbs (103 kg).
Maximum speed: approximately 62 (65) mph (100 [105] kmh).

Manufacturer: VEB Motorradwerk Zschopau, Zschopau/Erzgebirge.

MZ TS 250/1

Engine: 244 cc single cylinder two-stroke, maximum output 19 bhp SAE at 5,200 rpm. Bore and stroke 69×65 mm. Compression ratio 9.5:1. Central float carburettor. 50:1 petroil lubrication. Kick start.
Transmission: primary drive by gears; final by fully-enclosed chain. Five-speed gearbox. Wet multiplate clutch.
Ignition: battery and coil. 6v/40–45w dynamo.
Frame: parallel tubular.
Suspension: front, telescopic forks; rear, swinging arm with adjustable shock absorbers.

Tyres: front, 2.75×18; rear, 3.50×16.
Brakes: front, 160 mm drum; rear, 160 mm drum.
Tank capacity: 3.85 gallons (17.5 litres).
Weight: 287 lbs (130 kg).
Maximum speed: approximately 81 mph (130 kmh).

Manufacturer: VEB Motorradwerk Zschopau, Zschopau/Erzgebirge.

SIMSON S 50 B

Engine: 49.6 cc single cylinder two-stroke, maximum output 3.6 bhp SAE at 5,500 rpm. Bore and stroke 40×39.5 mm. Compression ratio 9.5:1. 16 mm BVF carburettor. 50:1 petroil lubrication. Kick start.
Transmission: primary drive by gears; final by fully-enclosed chain. Three-speed gearbox. Wet multiplate clutch.
Ignition: electronic. 6v.
Frame: tubular single beam.
Suspension: front, telescopic forks; rear, swinging arm.
Tyres: front, 2.75×20; rear, 2.75×20.
Brakes: front, 125 mm drum; rear, 125 mm drum.
Tank capacity: 2 gallons (9.5 litres).
Weight: 172 lbs (78 kg).
Maximum speed: approximately 37 mph (60 kmh).

Manufacturer: IFA-Kombinat VEB Fahrzeug-und-Jagdwaffenwerk; Ernst Thälmann, Suhl/Thür.

MOTOBÉCANE 51 VLC

Engine: 49.9 cc single cylinder two-stroke, maximum output 2.7 bhp (DIN) at 5,500 rpm. Bore and stroke 39×41.8 mm. Compression ratio 9:1. 13 mm Gurtner carburettor. Petroil lubrication. Pedal start.
Transmission: primary drive by belt; final by chain. Variomatic gear.
Ignition: Flywheel magneto. 6v/12w.
Frame: pressed steel.
Suspension: front, telescopic forks; rear, swinging arm.
Tyres: front, 2.25×17; rear, 2.25×17.

Brakes: front, 80 mm drum; rear, 80 mm drum.
Tank capacity: 0.8 gallons (3.65 litres).
Weight: 99 lbs (45 kg).
Maximum speed: approximately 31 mph (50 kmh).

Manufacturer: Motobécane SA, 16, rue Lesault–94500 Pantin

MOTOBÉCANE 95 TT

Engine: 49.9 cc single cylinder two-stroke, maximum output 1.85 bhp (DIN) at 4,350 rpm. Bore and stroke 39×41.8 mm. Compression ratio 9:1. 13 mm Gurtner carburettor. Petroil lubrication. Pedal start.
Transmission: primary drive by belt; final by chain. Variomatic gear.
Ignition: flywheel magneto 6v/18w.
Frame: tubular/pressed steel.
Suspension: front, telescopic forks; rear, swinging arm.
Tyres: front, 2.50×19; rear, 2.50×17.

Brakes: front, 100 mm drum; rear, 100 mm drum.
Tank capacity: 1.9 gallons (8.7 litres).
Weight: 139 lbs (63 kg).
Maximum speed: approximately 31 mph (50 kmh).

Manufacturer: Motobécane SA, 16, rue Lesault–93500 Pantin.

MOTOBÉCANE 125 LT 3

Engine: 124.9 cc two cylinder two-stroke, maximum output 16 bhp (DIN) at 7,500 rpm. Bore and stroke 43×43 mm. Compression ratio 10:1. Two 19 mm Gurtner carburettors. 24:1 petroil lubrication. Kick start.
Transmission: primary drive by gears; final by chain. Five-speed gearbox. Wet multiplate clutch.
Ignition: Thyristor electronic. 6v/35w.
Frame: tubular duplex cradle.
Suspension: front, telescopic forks; rear, Ceriani swinging arm.

Tyres: front, 2.50×17; rear, 3.00×17.
Brakes: front, 160 mm drum; rear, 160 mm drum.
Tank capacity: 2.9 gallons (13 litres).
Weight: 203 lbs (92 kg).
Maximum speed: approximately 80 mph (129 kmh).

Manufacturer: Motobécane SA, 16 rue Lesault, 93502 Pantin.

DUNSTALL SUZUKI GS 1000

Engine: 997 cc four cylinder double overhead camshaft, maximum output, bore and stroke not stated. Bore and stroke 70 × 66 mm. Compression ratio 10.5:1. Four carburettors. Wet sump lubrication. Kick/electric start.
Transmission: primary drive by straight-cut gears; final by chain. Five-speed gearbox. Wet multiplate clutch.
Ignition: battery and coil. 12v alternator.
Frame: tubular duplex cradle.
Suspension: front, telescopic forks; rear, swinging arm with adjustable shock absorbers.
Tyres: front, 4.10 × 19; rear, 4.25 × 18.
Brakes: front, discs; rear, disc.
Tank capacity: 3.7 gallons (17 litres).
Weight: 540 lbs. (245 kg).
Maximum speed: approximately 143 mph (230 kmh).

Manufacturer: Paul Dunstall Organisation Ltd., Crabtree Manorway, Belvedere, Kent.

FB-AJS ENDURO 250

Engine: 247 cc five port single cylinder two-stroke, maximum output not stated. Amal 34 mm carburettor. Petroil lubrication. Kick start.
Transmission: primary drive by chain; final by chain. Four-speed gearbox. All metal diaphragm clutch.
Ignition: electronic.
Frame: tubular duplex cradle.
Suspension: front, telescopic forks; rear, swinging arm with adjustable shock absorbers.
Tyres: front, 21 inch; rear, 18 inch.
Brakes front, drum; rear, drum.

Tank capacity: 2 gallons (9.1 litres).
Weight: 230 lbs (104 kg).
Maximum speed: approximately 80 mph (128 kmh).

Manufacturer: AJS of Andover, Goodworth Clatford, Andover, Hampshire.

FB-AJS MOTO-CROSS 360

Engine: 360 cc five port single cylinder two-stroke, maximum output not stated. Amal 38 mm carburettor. Petroil lubrication. Kick start.
Transmission: primary drive by chain; final by chain. Four-speed gearbox. All metal diaphragm clutch.
Ignition: electronic.
Frame: tubular duplex cradle.
Suspension: front, telescopic forks; rear, swinging arm with adjustable shock absorbers.
Tyres: front, 21 inch; rear, 18 inch.
Brakes: front, drum; rear, drum.

Tank capacity: 1.5 gallons (6.8 litres).
Weight: 230 lbs (104 kg).
Maximum speed: approximately 80 mph (128 kmh).

Manufacturer: AJS of Andover, Goodworth Clatford, Andover, Hampshire.

NVT RANGER

Engine: 49 cc single cylinder two-stroke, maximum output 1.3 bhp (DIN) at 4,500 rpm. Bore and stroke 40.4 × 39 mm. Compression ratio 7.8:1. Single carburettor. 20:1 petroil lubrication. Kick start.
Transmission: automatic single-speed drive.
Ignition: flywheel magneto.
Frame: single beam.
Suspension: front, telescopic forks; rear, cantilever springing.
Tyres: front, 2.75 × 14; rear, 2.75 × 17.
Brakes front, drum; rear, drum.
Tank capacity: 0.4 gallons (1.8 litres).

Weight: 89 lbs (40.3 kg).
Maximum speed: approximately 18 mph (28.9 kmh).

Manufacturer: NVT Motorcycles Ltd., Lynn Lane, Shenstone, Staffordshire.

QUASAR

Engine: 850 cc four cylinder four-stroke, maximum output 41 bhp (DIN) at 5,500 rpm. Bore and stroke 62.5×69.9 mm. Compression ratio 9:1. Single SU carburettor. Positive pump wet sump lubrication. Electric start.
Transmission: primary drive direct; final by shaft. Four-speed gearbox. Dry single plate clutch.
Ignition: battery, coil and distributor. 12v/330w alternator.
Frame: nylon coated tubular.
Suspension: front, pivoted fork; rear, swinging arm with gas shock absorbers.
Tyres: front, 4.25×18; rear, 4.25×18.
Brakes: front, 24 mm discs; rear, 24 mm disc.
Tank capacity: 3.75 gallons (17.06 litres).
Weight: 683 lbs (309.8 kg).
Maximum speed: approximately 100 mph (160.9 kmh).

Manufacturer: Wilson & Sons Ltd, Morley Road, Staple Hill, Bristol.

SILK 700 SPR PRODUCTION

Engine: 653 cc two cylinder two-stroke, maximum output 48 bhp (DIN) at 6,500 rpm. Bore and stroke 76 × 72 mm. Compression ratio 8:1. One 34 mm Amal carburettor. Positive pump lubrication. Kick start.
Transmission: primary drive by chain; final by chain. Four-speed gearbox. Wet multiplate clutch.
Ignition: electronic CDI. 12v/150w alternator.
Frame: tubular duplex.
Suspension: front, telescopic forks; rear, swinging arm with adjustable shock absorbers.

Tyres: front, 3.60 × 18; rear, 4.10 × 18.
Brakes front, 254 mm disc; rear, 180 mm drum.
Tank capacity: 4 gallons (18.2 litres).
Weight: 310 lbs (140.6 kg).
Maximum speed: approximately 112 mph (180.2 kmh).

Manufacturer: Silk Engineering (Derby) Ltd., Boar's Head Mill, Darley Abbey, Derby.

TRIUMPH BONNEVILLE 750 T140 V

Engine: 744 cc two cylinder overhead valve four-stroke, maximum output 50 bhp (DIN) at 6,750 rpm. Bore and stroke 76×82 mm. Compression ratio 7.9:1. Twin Amal 930 carburettors. Positive pump dry sump lubrication. Kick start.
Transmission: primary drive by chain; final by chain. Five-speed gearbox. Wet multiplate clutch.
Ignition: battery and coil. 12v crank-shaft alternator.
Frame: tubular duplex cradle.
Suspension: front, telescopic forks; rear, swinging arm with adjustable shock absorbers.
Tyres: front, 3.25×19; rear, 4.00×18.
Brakes: front, 254 mm disc; rear, 254 mm disc.
Tank capacity: 4 gallons (18.2 litres).
Weight: 395 lbs (179.1 kg).
Maximum speed: approximately 105 mph (168.9 kmh).

Manufacturer: Triumph Motorcycles (Meridan) Ltd., Alleley, Coventry.

TRIUMPH TIGER 750 TR7 RV

Engine: 744 cc twin cylinder overhead valve four-stroke, maximum output 43 bhp (DIN) at 6,200 rpm. Bore and stroke 76×82 mm. Compression ratio 7.9:1. Single Amal 930 carburettor. Positive pump dry sump lubrication. Kick start.
Transmission: primary drive by chain; final by chain. Five-speed gearbox. Wet multiplate clutch.
Ignition: battery and coil. 12v crankshaft alternator.
Frame: tubular duplex cradle.
Suspension: front, telescopic forks; rear, swinging arm with adjustable shock absorbers.
Tyres: front, 3.25×19; rear, 4.00×18.
Brakes: front, 254 mm disc; rear, 254 mm disc.
Tank capacity: 4 gallons (18.2 litres).
Weight: 413 lbs (187.3 kg).
Maximum speed: approximately 100 mph (160.9 kmh).

Manufacturer: Triumph Motorcycles (Meridan) Ltd., Alleley, Coventry.

LAMBRETTA 125/DL

Engine: 123 cc single cylinder two-stroke, maximum output 7.4 bhp (DIN) at 6,200 rpm. Bore and stroke 52×58 mm. Dell'Orto SH carburettor. Petroil lubrication. Kick start.
Transmission: primary drive by chain; final by direct drive from four speed gear box. Wet multiplate clutch.
Ignition: flywheel magneto.
Frame: tubular.
Suspension: front, trailing link; rear, swinging arm.
Tyres: front, 3.50×10; rear, 3.50×10.
Brakes: front, drum; rear, drum.

Tank capacity: 1.8 gallons (8.1 litres).
Weight: 231 lbs (105 kg).
Maximum speed: 59 mph (95 kmh).

Manufacturer: Scooters India.

LAMBRETTA 150/GP

Engine: 148 cc single cylinder two-stroke, maximum output 9.4 bhp (DIN) at 6,300 rpm. Bore and stroke 57×58 mm. Compression ratio 8.25:1. 22 mm Dell'Orto SH carburettor. 25:1 petroil lubrication. Kick start.
Transmission: primary drive by chain; final direct from four-speed gearbox. Wet multiplate clutch.
Ignition: flywheel magneto.
Frame: tubular.
Suspension: front, trailing link; rear, swinging arm.
Tyres: front, 3.50×10; rear, 3.50×10.
Brakes: front, drum; rear, drum.

Tank capacity: 1.9 gallons (8 litres).
Weight: 265 lbs (120 kg).
Maximum speed: approximately 63 mph (102 kmh).

Manufacturer: Scooters India.

LAMBRETTA 200/GP

Engine: 198 cc single cylinder two-stroke, maximum output 12.4 bhp (DIN) at 6,300 rpm. Bore and stroke 66×58 mm. Compression ratio 8.2:1. 22 mm Dell'Orto SH carburettor. 25:1 petroil lubrication. Kick start.
Transmission: primary drive by chain; final direct from four-speed gearbox. Wet multiplate clutch.
Ignition: flywheel magneto.
Frame: tubular.
Suspension: front, trailing link; rear, swinging arm.
Tyres: front, 3.50×10; rear, 3.50×10.
Brakes: front, drum; rear, drum.
Tank capacity: 1.9 gallons (8.6 litres).
Weight: 271 lbs (122 kg).
Maximum speed: approximately 71 mph (114 kmh).

Manufacturer: Scooters India.

ASPES JUMA 125 SPORT

Engine: 123.15 cc single cylinder two-stroke, maximum output 19.2 bhp (DIN) at 9,600 rpm. Bore and stroke 54×53.8 mm. Compression ratio 10.5:1. 30 mm Dell'Orto carburettor. 19:1 petroil lubrication. Kick start.
Transmission: primary drive by gears; final by chain. Six-speed gearbox. Wet multiplate clutch.
Ignition: Dansi electronic.
Frame: tubular duplex cradle.
Suspension: front, telescopic forks; rear, swinging arm.
Tyres: front, 2.50×18; rear, 3.00×18.
Brakes: front, disc; rear, drum.
Tank capacity: 2 gallons (9 litres).
Weight: 200 lbs (95 kg).
Maximum speed: approximately 84 mph (140 kmh).

Manufacturer: Sorrentino T & C, Fabbrica Moto-Aspes, Via Magenta 29, Gallarate (Varese).

ASPES NAVAHO SCRAMBLER 50cc

Engine: 49.6 cc single cylinder two-stroke, maximum output 1.5 bhp (DIN). Bore and stroke 38.8×42 mm. Compression ratio 11:1. Dell'Orto SHA 14-12 12mm carburettor.
Transmission: primary drive by gears; final by chain. Six-speed gearbox. Wet multiplate clutch.
Frame: tubular duplex cradle.
Suspension: front, telescopic forks; rear, hydraulic shock absorbers.
Tyres: not stated.
Brakes: front, drum; rear, drum.
Tank capacity: 1 gallon (4.5 litres).

Weight: 165 lbs (75 kg).
Maximum speed: approximately 29 mph (40 kmh).

Manufacturer: Sorrentino T. & C., Fabbrica Moto-Aspes, Via Magenta 29, Gallarate (VA).

ASPES HOPI 125 RGC

Engine: 123.15 cc single cylinder two-stroke, maximum output 21 bhp (DIN) at 9,500 rpm. Bore and stroke 54×53.8 mm. Compression ratio 11.5:1. 32 mm Dell'Orto PHB carburettor. 19:1 petroil lubrication. Kick start.
Transmission: primary drive by gears; final by chain. Six-speed gearbox. Wet multiplate clutch.
Ignition: Motoplat electronic.
Frame: tubular duplex cradle.
Suspension: front, Ceriani telescopic forks; rear, swinging arm with gas shock absorbers.
Tyres: front, 3.00×21; rear, 4.00×18.

Brakes: front, 125 mm drum; rear, 140 mm drum.
Tank capacity: 1.9 gallons (8.64 litres).
Weight: 220 lbs (100 kg).
Maximum speed: approximately 73 mph (117.4 kmh).

Manufacturer: Sorrentino T & C, Fabbrica Moto-Aspes, Via Magenta 29, Gallarate (Varese).

BENELLI 125 2C SE

Engine: 125 cc two cylinder two-stroke, maximum output 17 bhp (DIN) at 8,100 rpm. Bore and stroke 42.5×44 mm. Compression ratio 10:1. Two 19 mm Dell'Orto SHB carburettors. 25:1 petroil lubrication. Kick start.
Transmission: primary drive by gears; final by chain. Five-speed gearbox. Wet multiplate clutch.
Ignition: electronic. 6v.
Frame: tubular duplex cradle.
Suspension: front, telescopic forks; rear, swinging arm.
Tyres: front, 2.75×18; rear, 3.00×18.

Brakes: front, 260 mm disc; rear, 185 mm drum.
Tank capacity: 2.75 gallons (12.5 litres).
Weight: 249 lbs (113 kg).
Maximum speed: approximately 80 mph (130 kmh).

Manufacturer: Fratelli Benelli SpA, Via Mameli 22, Pesaro.

BENELLI 125 ENDURO

Engine: 121 cc single cylinder two-stroke, maximum output 15.4 bhp (DIN) at 7,800 rpm. Bore and stroke 56×49 mm. Compression ratio 9.5:1. Dell'Orto VHB 22 BS carburettor. Petroil lubrication. Kick start.
Transmission: primary drive by gears; final by chain. Five-speed gearbox.
Ignition: flywheel magneto with 6v 8Ah battery.
Frame: closed duplex frame.
Suspension: front, telescopic forks; rear, swinging arm.
Tyres: front, 2.50×21; rear, 3.50×18.

Brakes: front, 135 mm drum; rear, 135 mm drum.
Tank capacity: 1.9 gallons (8.5 litres).
Weight: 216 lbs (98 kg).
Maximum speed: 67 mph (110 kmh).

Manufacturer: Fratelli Benelli SpA, Via Mameli 22, Pesaro.

BENELLI 250 4

Engine: 231 cc four cylinder four-stroke, maximum output 26.6 bhp (DIN) at 10,500 rpm. Bore and stroke 44×38 mm. Compression ratio 11.5:1. Four carburettors. Kick/electric start.
Transmission: primary drive by chain; final by chain. Five-speed gearbox. Wet multiplate clutch.
Ignition: battery and coil. 12v/100w alternator dynamo.
Frame: tubular.
Suspension: front, telescopic forks; rear, swinging arm with adjustable shock absorbers.
Tyres: front, 3.00×18; rear, 3.25×18.

Brakes: front, 260 mm disc; rear, 158 mm drum.
Tank capacity: 2.5 gallons (11.5 litres).
Weight: 257 lbs (117 kg).
Maximum speed: approximately 93 mph (150 kmh).

Manufacturer: Fratelli Benelli SpA, Via Mameli 22, Pesaro.

BENELLI 250 2C ELETTRONICA

Engine: 232 cc two cylinder two-stroke, maximum output 32 bhp (DIN) at 8,000 rpm. Bore and stroke 56×47 mm. Compression ratio 10:1. Two 25 mm Dell'Orto VHB carburettors. 25:1 petroil lubrication. Kick start.
Transmission: primary drive by gears; final by chain. Five-speed gearbox. Wet multiplate clutch.
Ignition: transistor flywheel magneto. 6v.
Frame: tubular duplex cradle.
Suspension: front, telescopic forks; rear, swinging arm with adjustable shock absorbers.

Tyres: front, 3.00×18; rear, 3.25×18.
Brakes: front, 260 mm disc; rear, 185 mm drum.
Tank capacity: 2.75 gallons (12.5 litres).
Weight: 303 lbs (138 kg).
Maximum speed: approximately 86 mph (140 kmh).

Manufacturer: Fratelli Benelli SpA, Via Mameli 22, Pesaro.

BENELLI 354 SPORT

Engine: 345.57 cc four cylinder four-stroke, ohc, maximum output 38 bhp (DIN) at 10,200 rpm. Bore and stroke not stated. Compression ratio 10.4:1. Four Dell'Orto VHB 20D carburettors. Wet sump lubrication. Electric start.
Transmission: primary drive by chain; final by chain. Five-speed gearbox. Wet multiplate clutch.
Ignition: coil with 12v 15Ah battery.
Frame: tubular duplex cradle.
Suspension: front, telescopic forks; rear, swinging arm.
Tyres: front, 3.00×18; rear, 3.25×18.
Brakes: front, discs; rear, disc.
Tank capacity: 3.5 gallons (15.5 litres).
Weight: 370 lbs (168 kg).
Maximum speed: 100 mph (160 kmh).

Manufacturer: Fratelli Benelli SpA, Via Mameli 22, Pesaro.

BENELLI 500 LS

Engine: 498.5 cc four cylinder overhead camshaft four-stroke, maximum output 49 bhp (DIN) at 8,900 rpm. Bore and stroke 56×50.6 mm. Compression ratio 10.2:1. Wet sump lubrication. Electric start.
Transmission: mixed primary drive; final by chain. Five-speed gearbox. Wet multiplate clutch.
Ignition: CDI. 12v.
Frame: tubular duplex cradle.
Suspension: front, telescopic forks; rear, swinging arm.
Tyres: front, 3.00×18; rear, 3.50×18.
Brakes: front, 260 mm discs; rear, drum.
Tank capacity: 4.1 gallons (19 litres).
Weight: 419 lbs (183 kg).
Maximum speed: approximately 110 mph (180 kmh).

Manufacturer: Fratelli Benelli SpA, Via Mameli 22, Pesaro.

BENELLI 750/6

Engine: 747.7 cc six cylinder four-stroke, maximum output 75 bhp (DIN) at 9,000 rpm. Bore and stroke 56×50.6 mm. Compression ratio 9:1. Three 24 mm Dell'Orto VHB carburettors. Kick/electric start.
Transmission: mixed primary drive by chain; final by chain. Five-speed gearbox. Wet multiplate clutch.
Ignition: electronic. 12v.
Frame: tubular duplex cradle.
Suspension: front, telescopic forks; rear, swinging arm with adjustable shock absorbers.
Tyres: front, 3.50×18; rear, 4.00×18.
Brakes: front, 300 mm discs; rear, 200 mm drum.
Tank capacity: 4.8 gallons (22 litres).
Weight: 485 lbs (220 kg).
Maximum speed: approximately 124 mph (200 kmh).

Manufacturer: Fratelli Benelli SpA, Via Mameli 22, Pesaro.

BENELLI 900 16

Engine: 906 cc six cylinder four-stroke ohc, maximum output 80 bhp (DIN) at 8,000 rpm. Bore and stroke not stated. Compression ratio 9.4:1. Three VHB 24 Dell'Orto carburettors. Pump lubrication. Electric/kick start.
Transmission: primary drive by chain; final by chain. Five-speed gearbox. Dry multiple-disc clutch.
Ignition: Electronic by 12v 24Ah battery.
Frame: enclosed duplex cradle.
Suspension: front, telescopic forks; rear, swinging arm with adjustable shock-absorbers.
Tyres: front, 3.50×18; rear, 4.25×18.
Brakes: front, 300 mm discs; rear, 250 mm disc.
Tank capacity: 5 gallons (22 litres).
Weight: 485 lbs (220 kg).
Maximum speed: 127 mph (205 kmh).

Manufacturer: Fratelli Benelli SpA, Via Mameli 22, Pesaro.

CAGIVA SS-175

Engine: 174.15 cc single cylinder two-stroke, maximum output 15.5 bhp (DIN) at 6,750 rpm. Bore and stroke 61×59.6 mm. Compression ratio 10.7:1. 27 mm Dell'Orto VHB carburettor. Positive pump lubrication. Kick start.
Transmission: primary drive by gears; final by chain. Five-speed gearbox. Dry multiplate clutch.
Ignition: CDI 12v alternator.
Frame: tubular duplex cradle.
Suspension: front, telescopic forks; rear, swinging arm with adjustable shock absorbers.
Tyres: front, 3.25×19; rear, 4.00×18.

Brakes: front, 180 mm drum; rear, 180 mm drum.
Tank capacity: 2.8 gallons (13 litres).
Weight: 253 lbs (115 kg).
Maximum speed: approximately 73 mph (120 kmh).

Manufacturer: AMF Harley-Davidson Varese SpA, 21100 Schiranna (VA).

CAGIVA SST-250

Engine: 242.6 cc single cylinder two-stroke, maximum output 20.5 bhp (DIN) at 7,200 rpm. Bore and stroke 72×59 mm. Compression ratio 10.3:1. 32 mm Dell'Orto PHB carburettor. Positive pump lubrication. Kick start.
Transmission: primary drive by gears; final by chain. Five-speed gearbox. Dry multiplate clutch.
Ignition: CDI 12v alternator.
Frame: tubular duplex cradle.
Suspension: front, telescopic forks; rear, swinging arm with adjustable shock absorbers.
Tyres: front, 3.25×19; rear, 4.00×18.

Brakes: front, 220 mm disc; rear, 180 mm drum.
Tank capacity: 2.8 gallons (12 litres).
Weight: 259 lbs (118 kg).
Maximum speed: approximately 85 mph (135 kmh).

Manufacturer: AMF Harley-Davidson Varese SpA, 21100 Schiranna (VA).

CAGIVA HD SX 350

Engine: 341.8 cc single cylinder two-stroke, maximum output 28 bhp (DIN) at 7,100 rpm. Bore and stroke 80×68 mm. Compression ratio 9.6:1. Positive pump lubrication. Kick start.
Transmission: primary drive by gears; final by chain. Five-speed gearbox. Wet multiplate clutch.
Ignition: CDI 12v alternator.
Suspension: front, telescopic forks; rear, swinging arm.
Tyres: front, 3.00×21; rear, 4.00×18.
Brakes: front, 160 mm drum; rear, 160 mm drum.

Tank capacity: 2.7 gallons (12 litres).
Weight: 284 lbs (129 kg).
Maximum speed: approximately 84 mph (135 kmh).

Manufacturer: Cagiva Motor S.p.A. Varese, 21100 Schiranna (VA)

CAGIVA SST-350

Engine: 341.8 cc single cylinder two-stroke, maximum output 27 bhp (DIN) at 6,800 rpm. Bore and stroke 80×68 mm. Compression ratio 9.6:1. 34 mm carburettor. Positive pump lubrication. Kick start.
Transmission: primary drive by gears; final by chain. Five-speed gearbox. Wet multiplate clutch.
Ignition: not stated.
Frame: duplex cradle.
Suspension: front, telescopic forks; rear, swinging arm with adjustable shock absorbers.
Tyres: front, 3.25×19; rear, 4.00×18.

Brakes: front, 264 mm disc; rear, 160 mm drum.
Tank capacity: 3 gallons (14 litres).
Weight: 288 lbs (127 kg).
Maximum speed: approximately 88 mph (142 kmh).

Manufacturer: AMF Harley-Davidson Varese SpA, 21100 Schiranna (VA).

CIMATTI 86XL RADIAL 4M

Engine: 49 cc single cylinder two-stroke, maximum output not stated. Petroil lubrication. Kick start.
Transmission: four-speed gearbox.
Ignition: flywheel magneto.
Frame: open single tube.
Suspension: front, telescopic fork; rear, swinging arm.
Tyres: front, 2.75×16; rear, 3.25×16.
Brakes: front, 220 mm disc; rear, 118 mm disc.
Tank capacity: 0.6 gallons (2.8 litres).

Weight: 139 lbs (63 kg).
Maximum speed: not stated.

Manufacturer: Climatti Maro, Pioppe di Salvaro, Bologna.

CIMATTI PIPER V1 KS DE LUXE

Engine: 49.6 cc single cylinder two-stroke, maximum output not stated. Petroil lubrication. Kick start.
Transmission: single-speed automatic clutch.
Ignition: Flywheel magneto 6v 18w battery.
Frame: open single tube
Suspension: front, telescopic forks; rear, swinging arm.
Tyres: front, 2.50×16; rear, 2.50×16.
Brakes: front, drum; rear, drum.
Tank capacity: 0.45 gallons (2 litres).

Weight: 115 lbs (52 kg).
Maximum speed: not stated.

Manufacturer: Cimatti Marco, Pioppe di Salvaro, Bologna.

CIMATTI KAIMAN SUPER 6M RADIAL X21

Engine: 49.6 cc single cylinder two-stroke, maximum output 12 bhp (DIN) at 7,000 rpm. Bore and stroke 40×39 mm. Compression ratio 7:1. Dell'Orto VHB 14-14 carburettor. Petroil lubrication. Kick start.
Transmission: 6-speed gearbox with pedal control.
Ignition: electronic
Frame: tubular duplex cradle.
Suspension: front, telescopic forks; rear, swinging arm.
Tyres: front, 2.50×21; rear, 3.50×18.
Brakes: front, 125 mm drum; rear, 125 mm drum.
Tank capacity: 1.2 gallons (5.5 litres).
Weight: 181 lbs (82 kg).
Maximum speed: not stated

Manufacturer: Cimatti Marco, Pioppe di Salvaro, Bologna.

DUCATI 500 GTV

Engine: 496.9 cc two cylinder four-stroke, maximum output 72 bhp (DIN) at 9,500 rpm. Bore and stroke 78 × 52 mm. Compression ratio 10:1. Two 30 mm Dell'Orto PHF carburettors. Positive pump lubrication. Electric start.
Transmission: primary drive by gears; final by chain. Five-speed gearbox. Wet multiplate clutch.
Ignition: 12v/150w alternator.
Frame: tubular duplex cradle.
Suspension: front, telescopic forks; rear, swinging arm with adjustable shock absorbers.
Tyres: front, 3.25 × 18; rear, 3.50 × 18.
Brakes: front, 260 mm discs; rear, 260 mm disc.
Tank capacity: 3 gallons (14 litres).
Weight: 399 lbs (181 kg).
Maximum speed: approximately 108 mph (175 kmh).

Manufacturer: Ducati Meccanica SpA, Via Ducati 3, Bologna.

DUCATI 900 SPORT DESMO

Engine: 863.9 cc two cylinder (Desmodronic) overhead camshaft four-stroke, maximum output not stated. Bore and stroke 86×74.4 mm. Compression ratio 9.4:1. Two 32 mm Dell'Orto PHF carburettors. Positive pump lubrication. Kick/electric start.
Transmission: primary drive by gears; final by chain. Five-speed gearbox. Wet multiplate clutch.
Ignition: electronic. 12v/200w alternator.
Frame: tubular cradle.
Suspension: front, telescopic forks; rear, swinging arm with adjustable shock absorbers.
Tyres: front, 3.50×18; rear 4.25×18.
Brakes: front, 280 mm discs; rear, 280 mm disc.
Tank capacity: 3.3 gallons (15 litres).
Weight: 475 lbs (216 kg).
Maximum speed: approximately 121 mph (195 kmh).

Manufacturer: Ducati Meccanica SpA, Via Ducati 3, Bologna.

DUCATI SUPER SPORT DESMO

Engine: 863.9 cc two cylinder four-stroke, maximum output 72 bhp (DIN) at 9,500 rpm. Desmodronic positive timing to overhead valve. Bore and stroke 86 × 74.4 mm. Compression ratio 9.5:1. Two 40 mm Dell'Orto PHH carburettors. Wet sump lubrication. Kick start.
Transmission: primary drive by gears; final by chain. Five-speed gearbox. Wet multiplate clutch.
Ignition: electronic. 200w alternator.
Frame: tubular cradle.
Suspension: front, telescopic forks; rear, swinging arm with adjustable shock absorbers.
Tyres: front, 3.50 × 18; rear, 4.72 × 18.
Brakes: front, 280 mm discs; rear, 223 mm disc.
Tank capacity: 4 gallons (18 litres).
Weight: 414 lbs (188 kg).
Maximum speed: approximately 140 mph (225 kmh).

Manufacturer: Ducati Meccanica SpA, Via Ducati 3, Bologna.

FANTIC CABALLERO 50cc REG. CASA (SUPER 6M)

Engine: 49.6 cc single cylinder two-stroke, maximum output not stated. Bore and stroke 38.8×42 mm. Compression ratio 12:1. Dell'Orto SHA 14-12 carburettor. Petroil lubrication. Kick start.
Transmission: primary drive by gears; final by chain. Six-speed gearbox. Wet multiplate clutch.
Ignition: electronic.
Frame: tubular duplex cradle.
Suspension: front, telescopic forks; rear, swinging arm, adjustable to five positions.
Tyres: front, 2.50×21; rear, 3.50×18.

Brakes: front, 124 (123) mm conical drum; rear, 124 (123) mm conical drum.
Tank capacity: 1.4 gallons (6.5 litres).
Weight: 172 lbs (165 kg) (78 [75] kg).
Maximum speed: not stated.

Manufacturer: Fantic Motor, SpA, 22061 Barzago, Como.

GARELLI RGS 50

Engine: 49.9 cc single cylinder two-stroke, maximum output 1.5 bhp (DIN) at 4,800 rpm. Bore and stroke 40×39.6 mm. Compression ratio 8:1. Petroil lubrication.
Transmission: primary drive by gears; final by chain. Five-speed gearbox. Wet multiplate clutch.
Ignition: Magneto 6V 18W flywheel.
Frame: tubular duplex cradle.
Suspension: front, telescopic forks; at rear, swinging arm adjustable to four positions.
Tyres: front, 2.50×21; rear, 3.00×18.
Brakes: 124 mm drum.

Tank capacity: 1.5 gallons (6.7 litres).
Weight: 163 lbs (74 kg).
Maximum speed: 25 mph (40 kmh).

Manufacturer: Agrati-Garelli Monticello B (Como).

GARELLI KL 50 5V

Engine: 49.6 cc single cylinder two-stroke, maximum output 3 bhp (DIN) at 6,000 rpm. Bore and stroke 40×39.6 mm. Compression ratio 12:1. Dell'Orto SHB 18/12B carburettor. 20:1 petroil lubrication. Kick start.
Transmission: primary drive by gears; final by chain. Five-speed gearbox. Wet multiplate clutch.
Ignition: flywheel magneto electronic ignition.
Frame: tubular duplex cradle.
Suspension: front, telescopic forks; rear, swinging arm.
Tyres: front, 2.50×19; rear, 2.50×17.

Brakes: front, drum; rear, drum.
Tank capacity: 1.5 gallons (6.8 litres).
Weight: 167 lbs (75.7 kg).
Maximum speed: approximately 25 mph (40 kmh).

Manufacturer: Agrati-Garelli, Monticello B., (Como).

GILERA 50 V ENDURO

Engine: 49.8 cc single cylinder two-stroke, maximum output 1.4 bhp (DIN) at 4,500 rpm. Bore and stroke 38.4×43 mm. Compression ratio 6.35:1. 14.9 mm Dell'Orto SHA carburettor. Kick start.
Transmission: primary drive by gears; final by chain. Five-speed gearbox.
Ignition: flywheel magneto. 6v/18w.
Frame: tubular duplex cradle.
Suspension: front, telescopic forks; rear, swinging arm.
Tyres: front, 2.50×19; rear, 3.00×17.
Brakes: front, drum; rear, drum.

Tank capacity: 1.5 gallons (7 litres).
Weight: 154 lbs (70 kg).
Maximum speed: approximately 25 mph (40 kmh).

Manufacturer: Piaggio & C., Azienda Gilera, Arcore (Mi).

GILERA 125 5V ARCORE

Engine: 124.4 cc single cylinder four-stroke, maximum output 12.4 bhp (DIN) at 8,500 rpm. Bore and stroke 60×44 mm. Compression ratio 10:1. 22 mm Dell'Orto VHB carburettor. Kick start.
Transmission: primary drive by gears; final by chain. Five-speed gearbox.
Ignition: flywheel magneto.
Frame: tubular duplex cradle.
Suspension: front, telescopic forks; rear, swinging arm.
Tyres: front, 2.75×18; rear, 3.00×18.
Brakes: front, drum; rear, drum.

Tank capacity: 2.4 gallons (11 litres).
Weight: 244 lbs (111 kg).
Maximum speed: approximately 70 mph (112 kmh).

Manufacturer: Piaggio & C., Azienda Gilera, Arcore (Mi).

GILERA 125 GR 1

Engine: 122.5 cc single cylinder two-stroke, maximum output 14.5 bhp (DIN) at 7,200 rpm. Bore and stroke 57×48 mm. Compression ratio 10:1. 24 mm Dell'Orto VHB carburettor. Kick start.
Transmission: primary drive by gears; final by chain. Five-speed gearbox.
Ignition: flywheel magneto.
Frame: tubular duplex cradle.
Suspension: front, telescopic forks; rear, swinging arm.
Tyres: front, 2.75×21; rear, 3.00×18.
Brakes: front, drum; rear, drum.

Tank capacity: 1.5 gallons (6.8 litres).
Weight: 220 lbs (100 kg).
Maximum speed: approximately 66 mph (106 kmh).

Manufacturer: Piaggio & C., Azienda Gilera, Arcore (Mi).

GILERA TG 1

Engine: 122.5 cc single cylinder two-stroke, maximum output 14.5 bhp (DIN) at 7,200 rpm. Bore and stroke 57×48 mm. Compression ratio 12:1. 24 mm Dell'Orto VHB carburettor. 24:1 petroil lubrication. Kick start.
Transmission: primary drive by gears; final by chain. Five-speed gearbox. Wet multiplate clutch.
Ignition: electronic.
Frame: duplex cradle.
Suspension: front, telescopic forks; rear, swinging arm.
Tyres: front, 2.75×18; rear, 3.25×18.
Brakes: front, disc; rear, drum.
Tank capacity: 2.1 gallons (9.8 litres).
Weight: 224 lbs (102 kg).
Maximum speed: approximately 68.3 mph (110 kmh).

Manufacturer: Piaggio & C., Azienda Gilera, Arcore (Mi).

ITALJET BUCCANEER 125

Engine: 124.8 cc two cylinder two-stroke, maximum output 18 bhp (DIN) at 9,500 rpm. Bore and stroke 43×43 mm. Compression ratio 6.8:1. Two concentric carburettors. Positive pump lubrication. Kick start.
Transmission: primary drive by gears; final by chain. Five-speed gearbox.
Ignition: electronic.
Frame: tubular duplex cradle.
Suspension: front, telescopic forks; rear, swinging arm.
Tyres: front, 2.75×19; rear, 3.50×18.
Brakes: front, disc; rear, drum.
Tank capacity: 2.75 gallons (12.5 litres).
Weight: 250 lbs (113 kg).
Maximum speed: approximately 80 mph (130 kmh).

Manufacturer: Italjet, Via Palazzetto, San Lazzaro di Savena (Bo).

LAVERDA 125 CR

Engine: 124 cc single cylinder two-stroke, maximum output not stated. Bore and stroke 55 × 52 mm. Compression ratio 13.5:1. 32 mm Dell'Orto carburettor. 24:1 petroil lubrication. Kick start.
Transmission: primary drive by gears; final by chain. Six-speed gearbox. Wet multiplate clutch.
Ignition: Motoplat electronic.
Frame: tubular cradle.
Suspension: front, Marzocchi telescopic forks; rear, swinging arm with gas shock absorbers.
Tyres: front, 3.00 × 21; rear, 4.00 × 18.
Brakes front, drum conical; rear, drum conical.
Tank capacity: 2.09 gallons (9.5 litres).

Weight: not available.
Maximum speed: not stated.

Manufacturer: Moto Laverda, Breganze (Vicenza).

LAVERDA 250 REGOLARITA

Engine: 245 cc single cylinder two-stroke, maximum output 28 bhp (DIN). Bore and stroke 69.5 × 64.5 mm. Compression ratio 12.3:1. Mikuni carburettor. 24:1 petroil lubrication. Kick start.
Transmission: primary drive by gears; final by chain. Five-speed gearbox. Dry multiplate clutch.
Ignition: Motoplat electronic.
Frame: tubular cradle.
Suspension: front, Ceriani telescopic forks; rear, swinging arm with gas shock absorbers.
Tyres: front, 3.00 × 21; rear, 4.00 × 18.
Brakes: front, 180 mm Grimeca drum; rear, 180 mm Grimeca drum.
Tank capacity: 2 gallons (9.5 litres).

Weight: 235 lbs (107 kg).
Maximum speed: approximately 77 mph (123.9 kmh).

Manufacturer: Moto Laverda, Breganze (Vicenza).

LAVERDA 350

Engine: 344.5cc two-cylinder four-stroke, ohc. Four valves per cylinder. Maximum output not stated. Bore and stroke 60×61.6 mm. Compression ratio 8.7:1. Two Dell'Orto PHBL 24 B carburettors. Wet sump lubrication. Electric start.
Transmission: primary drive by gears; final by chain. Six-speed gearbox. Wet multiple plate clutch.
Ignition: electronic.
Frame: tubular duplex cradle.
Suspension: front, telescopic fork; rear, swinging arm.
Tyres: front, 90/90 S × 18; rear, 110/90 H × 18.
Brakes: front, 260 mm discs; rear, 260 mm disc.
Tank capacity: 3.2 gallons (14.3 litres).
Weight: 379 lbs (172 kg).
Maximum speed: approximately 90 mph (145 kmh).

Manufacturer: Moto Laverda, Breganze (Vicenza).

LAVERDA 500

Engine: 497 cc two cylinder double overhead camshaft four-stroke, maximum output not stated. Bore and stroke 72 × 61 mm. Two 32 mm Dell'Orto PHF carburettors. Wet sump lubrication.
Transmission: primary drive by gears; final by chain. Six-speed gearbox. Wet multiplate clutch.
Ignition: electronic Bosch. 12v/150w dynamo.
Frame: tubular cradle.
Suspension: front, telescopic forks; rear, swinging arm with adjustable Marzocchi shock absorbers.
Tyres: front, 3.93 × 18; rear, 3.93 × 18.
Brakes: front, 260 mm discs; rear 260 mm disc.
Tank capacity: 3 gallons (14.5 litres).
Weight: 379 lbs. (172 kg).
Maximum speed: approximately 104 mph (167 kmh).

Manufacturer: Moto Laverda, Breganze (Vicenza).

LAVERDA 1000

Engine: 980.76 cc three cylinder double overhead camshaft four-stroke, maximum output 80 bhp (DIN) at 7,250 rpm. Bore and stroke 75 × 74 mm. Compression ratio 9:1. Three 32 mm Dell'Orto PHF carburettors. Wet sump lubrication. Radiator for oil cooling. Electric start.
Transmission: primary drive by triplex chain; final by chain. Five-speed gearbox. Wet multiplate clutch.
Ignition: Bosch electronic CDI. 12v.
Frame: tubular duplex cradle.
Suspension: front, Ceriani telescopic forks; rear, swinging arm with adjustable shock absorbers.
Tyres: front, 4.10 × 18 inch; rear, 4.25 × 18.
Brakes front, 280 mm discs; rear, 280 mm disc.
Tank capacity: 4.5 gallons (20.5 litres).
Weight: 486 lbs (220 kg).
Maximum speed: approximately 140 mph (225 kmh).

Manufacturer: Moto Laverda, Breganze (Vicenza).

LAVERDA 1200

Engine: 1116 cc three cylinder double overhead camshaft four-stroke, maximum output 97 bph (DIN). Bore and stroke 80 × 74 mm. Compression ratio 9:1. Three 32 mm Dell'Orto PHF carburettors. Radiator-cooled lubrication. Electric start.
Transmission: primary drive by triplex chain; final by chain. Five-speed gearbox.
Ignition: electronic. 12v.
Frame: tubular duplex cradle.
Suspension: front, telescopic forks; rear, swinging arm with hydraulic shock absorbers.
Tyres: front, 4.10 × 18; rear, 4.25 × 18.
Brakes: front, 280 mm discs; rear, 280 mm disc.
Tank capacity: 4.4 gallons (20 litres).
Weight: 513 lbs (232 kg).
Maximum speed: approximately 135 mph (217 kmh).

Manufacturer: Moto Laverda, Breganze (Vicenza).

MOTO GUZZI 250 TS-FD

Engine: 231.4 cc two cylinder two-stroke, maximum output 30 bhp (DIN) at 8,000 rpm. Bore and stroke 56 × 47 mm. Compression ratio 10:1. Two 25 mm Dell'Orto VHB carburettors. 19:1 petroil lubrication. Kick start.
Transmission: primary drive by gears; final by chain. Five-speed gearbox. Wet multiplate clutch.
Ignition: electronic. 6v.
Frame: tubular duplex cradle.
Suspension: front, telescopic forks; rear, swinging arm.
Tyres: front, 3.00 × 18; rear, 3.25 × 18.
Brakes front, 260 mm disc; rear, 160 mm drum.
Tank capacity: 3.7 gallons (17 litres).
Weight: 310 lbs (137 kg).
Maximum speed: approximately 86 mph (140 kmh).

Manufacturer: Moto Guzzi, SEIMM, Mandello del Lario (Como).

MOTO GUZZI 254

Engine: 231.1 cc four cylinder overhead camshaft four-stroke, maximum output 26.6 bhp (DIN) at 10,500 rpm. Bore and stroke 44 × 38 mm. Compression ratio 11.5:1. Electric start.
Transmission: gear primary drive; final by chain. Five-speed gearbox. Wet multiplate clutch.
Ignition: battery and coil. 12v/200w alternator.
Frame: tubular cradle.
Suspension: front, telescopic forks; rear, swinging arm.
Tyres: front, 3.00 × 18; rear, 3.25 × 18.
Brakes: front, disc; rear, drum.
Tank capacity: 2.5 gallons (11.5 litres).
Weight: 263 lbs (117 kg).
Maximum speed: approximately 94 mph (140 kmh).

Manufacturer: Moto Guzzi, SEIMM, Mandello del Lario (Como).

MOTO GUZZI 850 LE MANS II

Engine: 844.05 cc two cylinder four-stroke, maximum output 80 bhp (DIN) at 7,600 rpm. Bore and stroke 83×78 mm. Compression ratio 10.2:1. Two 36 mm carburettors. Wet sump lubrication. Electric start.
Transmission: primary drive by gears; final by shaft. Five-speed gearbox.
Ignition: battery and coil. 12v alternator.
Frame: tubular duplex cradle.
Suspension: front, telescopic forks; rear, swinging arm.
Tyres: front, 3.50×18; rear, 4.10×18.
Brakes: front, 300 mm discs; rear, 242 mm disc.
Tank capacity: 5 gallons (22.5 litres).
Weight: 432 lbs (196 kg).
Maximum speed: approximately 143 mph (230 kmh).

Manufacturer: Moto Guzzi, SEIMM, Mandello del Lario (Como).

MOTO GUZZI 1000 SP

Engine: 949 cc two cylinder four-stroke, maximum output 71 bhp (DIN) at 6,500 rpm. Bore and stroke 88×78 mm. Compression ratio 9.2:1. Two carburettors. Electric start.
Transmission: primary drive by gears; final by shaft. Five-speed gearbox.
Ignition: battery and coil. 12v/350w.
Frame: tubular duplex cradle.
Suspension: front, telescopic forks; rear, swinging arm.
Tyres: front, 3.50×18; rear, 4.10×18.
Brakes: front, discs; rear, disc.
Tank capacity: 5.3 gallons (24 litres).
Weight: 463 lbs (210 kg).
Maximum speed: approximately 124 mph (200 kmh).

Manufacturer: Moto Guzzi, SEIMM, Mandello del Lario (Como).

ITALY

MOTO MORINI 250

Engine: 239.29 cc single cylinder
four-stroke, maximum output 19.5
bhp (DIN) at 7,000 rpm. Bore and
stroke 69×64 mm. Compression
ratio 9.5:1. 26 mm VHB carburettor.
Positive pump wet sump
lubrication. Kick start.
Transmission: primary drive by
gears; final by chain. Five-speed
gearbox. Wet multiplate clutch.
Ignition: electronic. 6v.
Frame: tubular duplex cradle.
Suspension: front, telescopic
forks; rear, swinging arm.
Tyres: front, 2.75×18; rear,
3.00×18.
Brakes: front, 260 mm disc; rear,
180 mm drum.
Tank capacity: 2.7 gallons
(12 litres).
Weight: 266 lbs (121 kg).
Maximum speed: approximately
83 mph (135 kmh).

Manufacturer: Moto Morini, Via A. Bergami 7, Bologna.

MOTO MORINI 500

Engine: 478.6 cc two cylinder four-stroke,
maximum output 46 bhp (SAE) at 7,500 rpm.
Bore and stroke 69×64 mm. Compression ratio
11.2:1. 26 mm Dell'Orto carburettors.
Transmission: primary drive by gears; final
by chain. Five-speed gearbox. Dry multiplate
clutch.
Ignition: electronic. 12v.
Frame: duplex cradle.
Suspension: front, telescopic forks; rear,
swinging arm.
Tyres: front, 90/90×18; rear, 3.50H×18.
Brakes: front, 260 mm discs; rear, 260 mm
disc.
Tank capacity: 3.5 gallons (16 litres).
Weight: 367 lbs (160 kg).
Maximum speed: approximately 110 mph
(177 kmh).

Manufacturer: Moto Morini, Via A. Bergami 7, Bologna.

MOTO MORINI 3½ SPORT

Engine: 344 cc two cylinder four-stroke, maximum output 39 bhp (SAE) at 8,500 rpm. Bore and stroke 62×57 mm. Compression ratio 11:1. Two 25 mm Dell'Orto VHB carburettors. Kick start.
Transmission: primary drive by gears; final by chain. Six-speed gearbox. Dry multiplate clutch.
Ignition: electronic. 12v.
Frame: duplex cradle.
Suspension: front, telescopic forks; rear, swinging arm.
Tyres: front, 3.25×18; rear, 4.10×18.
Brakes: front, 260 mm disc; rear, 180 mm drum.
Tank capacity: 3 gallons (14 litres).
Weight: 343 lbs (156 kg).
Maximum speed: approximately 108 mph (175 kmh).

Manufacturer: Moto Morini, Via A. Bergami 7, Bologna.

VESPA 125 PRIMAVERA

Engine: 121.16 cc single cylinder two-stroke, maximum output not stated. Bore and stroke 55×51 mm. Dell'Orto carburettor. 50:1 petroil lubrication. Kick start.
Transmission: primary drive by gears; final by direct drive. Four-speed gearbox. Wet multiplate clutch.
Ignition: flywheel magneto. 6v/50w.
Frame: monocoque pressed steel.
Suspension: front and rear, helical springs with double acting hydraulic dampers.
Tyres: front, 3.00×10; rear, 3.00×10.

Brakes: front, drum; rear, drum.
Tank capacity: 1.8 gallons (8.1 litres).
Weight: 175 lbs (79.3 kg).
Maximum speed: approximately 56 mph (90 kmh).

Manufacturer: Piaggio & C, Via Cecchi 6, Genoa.

VESPA P 200 E

Engine: 197.97 cc single cylinder two-stroke, maximum output 9.8 bhp (DIN). Bore and stroke 66.5×57 mm. Compression ratio not stated. 24 mm Dell'Orto SI carburettor. 49:1 petroil lubrication. Kick start.
Transmission: primary drive by gears; final by direct drive. Four-speed gearbox. Wet multiplate clutch.
Ignition: flywheel magneto. 6v/50w.
Frame: monocoque pressed steel.
Suspension: front, trailing link; rear, swinging arm.
Tyres: front, 3.50×10; rear, 3.50×10.

Brakes: front, drum; rear, drum.
Tank capacity: 1.7 gallons (8 litres).
Weight: 214 lbs (105 kg).
Maximum speed: approximately 68 mph (110 kmh).

Manufacturer: Piaggio & C, Via Cecchi 6, Genoa.

HONDA CB 125 T1

Engine: 124cc single cylinder four-stroke. Maximum output 14 bhp (DIN) at 10,000 rpm. Bore and stroke 56.5×49.5 mm. Compression ratio 9.4:1. 22 mm carburettor. Kick start.
Transmission: primary drive by gears; final by chain. Five-speed gearbox. Wet multiplate clutch.
Ignition: 75W generator.
Frame: single tube.
Suspension: front, telescopic fork; rear, swinging arm.
Tyres: front, 2.75×18; rear, 3.00×17.
Brakes: front, 240 mm disc; rear, 110 mm drum.
Tank capacity: 2 gallons (9.5 litres).
Weight: 220 lbs (100 kg).
Maximum speed: 74.5 mph (120 kmh).

Manufacturer: Honda Motor Co. Ltd., Tokyo.

HONDA XL 125 S

Engine: 124cc single cylinder four-stroke, ohc. Maximum output 146 bhp (DIN) at 10,000 rpm. Bore and stroke 56×49.6 mm. Compression ratio 9.4:1. Dell'Orto VHBZ 22 GS carburettor. Kick start.
Transmission: primary drive by gears; final by chain. Five-speed gearbox. Multiplate clutch.
Frame: single tube.
Suspension: front, telescopic fork; rear, swinging arm.
Tyres: front, 2.75×18; rear, 3.00×17.
Brakes: front, disc; rear, drum.
Tank capacity: 2 gallons (9.5 litres).

Weight: 223 lbs (101 kg).
Maximum speed: 73 mph (120 kmh).

Manufacturer: Honda Motor Co. Ltd., Tokyo.

HONDA CB 250 N

Engine: 249 cc twin cylinder overhead camshaft (3 valve) four-stroke, maximum output 27 bhp (DIN) at 10,000 rpm. Bore and stroke 62×41.4 mm. Compression ratio 9.4:1. Twin CV type 28 mm carburettors. Positive pump wet sump lubrication. Kick/electric start.
Transmission: primary drive by gears; final by chain. Six-speed gearbox. Wet multiplate clutch.
Ignition: CDI. 12v/130w alternator.
Frame: diamond type.
Suspension: front, telescopic

forks; rear, swinging arm with adjustable shock absorbers.
Tyres: front, 3.60×19; rear, 4.10×18.
Brakes: front, discs; rear, drum.
Tank capacity: 3.1 gallons (14 litres).
Weight: 367 lbs (166 kg).
Maximum speed: approximately 90 mph (145 kmh).

Manufacturer: Honda Motor Co. Ltd., Tokyo.

HONDA CB 400 N

Engine: 395 cc twin cylinder overhead camshaft (3 valves) four-stroke, maximum output 43 bhp (DIN) at 9,500 rpm. Bore and stroke 70.5×50.5 mm. Compression ratio 9.3:1. Two CV type 32 mm carburettors. Positive pump wet sump lubrication. Kick/electric start.
Transmission: primary drive by gears; final by chain. Six-speed gearbox. Wet multiplate clutch.
Ignition: CDI. 12v/150w alternator.
Frame: diamond type.
Suspension: front, telescopic forks; rear, swinging arm with adjustable shock absorbers.
Tyres: front, 3.60×19; rear, 4.10×18.
Brakes: front, discs; rear, drum.
Tank capacity: 3.1 gallons (14 litres).
Weight: 377 lbs (171 kg).
Maximum speed: approximately 108 mph (175 kmh).

Manufacturer: Honda Motor Co. Ltd., Tokyo.

HONDA CX 500

Engine: 497 cc two cylinder water-cooled four-stroke, maximum output 50 bhp (DIN) at 9,000 rpm. Bore and stroke 78×52 mm. Two carburettors. Wet sump lubrication. Electric start.
Transmission: primary drive by gears; final by shaft. Five-speed gearbox.
Ignition: electronic CDI. 12v.
Frame: diamond integral with engine.
Suspension: front, telescopic forks; rear, swinging arm.
Tyres: front, 3.25×19; rear, 3.75×18.
Brakes: front, discs; rear, drum.
Tank capacity: 3.7 gallons (17 litres).
Weight: 446 lbs (200 kg).
Maximum speed: approximately 112 mph (180 kmh).

Manufacturer: Honda Motor Co. Ltd., Tokyo.

HONDA CB 750 F2

Engine: 736 cc four cylinder four-stroke, maximum output 67 bhp (DIN) at 8,500 rpm. Bore and stroke 61×63 mm. Compression ratio 9:1. Four 26 mm Keihin carburettors. Positive pump wet sump lubrication. Kick/electric start.
Transmission: primary drive by chain; final by chain. Five-speed gearbox. Wet multiplate clutch.
Ignition: battery and coil. 12v/210w alternator.
Frame: tubular duplex cradle.
Suspension: front, telescopic forks; rear, swinging arm.
Tyres: front, 3.25×19; rear, 4.00×18.
Brakes: front, 296 mm discs; rear, 296 mm disc.
Tank capacity: 3.7 gallons (17 litres).
Weight: 542 lbs (246 kg).
Maximum speed: approximately 118 mph (189 kmh).

Manufacturer: Honda Motor Co. Ltd., Tokyo.

HONDA GL 1000 GOLD WING

Engine: 999 cc four cylinder water-cooled four-stroke, maximum output 80 bhp (DIN) at 7,500 rpm. Bore and stroke 72×61.4 mm. Compression ratio 9:1. Four 32 mm Keihin carburettors. Wet sump lubrication. Electric start.
Transmission: primary drive by chain; final by shaft. Five-speed gearbox. Wet multiplate clutch.
Ignition: battery and coil. 12v/300w.
Frame: tubular duplex cradle.
Suspension: front, telescopic forks; rear, swinging arm.
Tyres: front, 3.50×19; rear, 4.50×17.
Brakes: front, discs; rear, disc.
Tank capacity: 4.2 gallons (19 litres).
Weight: 635 lbs (290 kg).
Maximum speed: approximately 125 mph (200 kmh).

Manufacturer: Honda Motor Co. Ltd., Tokyo.

HONDA CB 900 FZ

Engine: 901 cc four cylinder four-stroke, dohc, maximum output 95 bhp (DIN) at 9,000 rpm. Bore and stroke 64.5×69 mm. Compression ratio 8.8:1. Four 32 mm carburettors. Electric start.
Transmission: primary drive by chain; final by chain. Five-speed gearbox. Wet multiplate clutch.
Ignition: electronic.
Frame: tubular duplex cradle.
Suspension: front, telescopic forks; rear, swinging arm with shock absorbers.
Tyres: front, 3.25×19; rear, 4.00×18.
Brakes: front, 276 mm discs; rear, 296 mm disc.
Tank capacity: 4 gallons (20 litres).
Weight: 511 lbs (232 kg).
Maximum speed: 133.5 mph (215 kmh).

Manufacturer: Honda Motor Co. Ltd., Tokyo.

HONDA CBX 1000

Engine: 1047 cc six cylinder double overhead camshaft four-stroke, maximum output 105 bhp (DIN) at 9,000 rpm. Four valves per cylinder. Bore and stroke 64.5×63.4 mm. Compression ratio 9.3:1. Six 26 mm Keihin VB carburettors. Wet sump lubrication. Electric start.
Transmission: primary drive by chain; final by chain. Five-speed gearbox. Wet multiplate clutch.
Ignition: electronic. 12v.
Frame: diamond construction.
Suspension: front, telescopic forks; rear, swinging arm with adjustable shock absorbers.
Tyres: front, 3.50×19; rear, 4.25×18.
Brakes: front, discs; rear, disc.
Tank capacity: 4.4 gallons (20 litres).
Weight: 546 lbs (247 kg).
Maximum speed: approximately 140 mph (225 kmh).

Manufacturer: Honda Motor Co. Ltd., Tokyo.

KAWASAKI KH 125

Engine: 124 cc single cylinder two-stroke, maximum output 14.5 bhp (DIN) at 7,500 rpm. Bore and stroke 56×50.6 mm. Compression ratio 7:1. 24 mm Mikuni carburettor. Positive pump lubrication. Kick start.
Transmission: primary drive by gears; final by chain. Six-speed gearbox. Wet multiplate clutch.
Ignition: flywheel magneto.
Frame: tubular duplex cradle.
Suspension: front, telescopic forks; rear, swinging arm.
Tyres: front, 2.75×18; rear, 3.00×18.
Brakes: front, 190 mm disc; rear, 110 mm drum.
Tank capacity: 2.5 gallons (11.5 litres).
Weight: 233 lbs (126 kg).
Maximum speed: approximately 73 mph (117 kmh).

Manufacturer: Kawasaki Heavy Industries Ltd., Motorcycle Division, World Trade Centre Building, Tokyo.

KAWASAKI Z 200

Engine: 198 cc single cylinder four-stroke, maximum output 18 bhp (DIN) at 8,000 rpm. Bore and stroke 66×58 mm. Compression ratio 9:1. 26 mm Keihin carburettor. Kick/electric start.
Transmission: primary drive by gears; final by chain. Five-speed gearbox. Wet multiplate clutch.
Ignition: battery and coil.
Frame: tubular cradle.
Suspension: front, telescopic forks; rear, swinging arm.
Tyres: front, 2.75×18; rear, 3.25×17.
Brakes: front, 206 mm disc; rear, 130 mm drum.
Tank capacity: 1.9 gallons (8.8 litres).
Weight: 277 lbs (126.6 kg).
Maximum speed: approximately 80 mph (128 kmh).

Manufacturer: Kawasaki Heavy Industries Ltd., Motorcycle Division, World Trade Centre Building, Tokyo.

KAWASAKI Z 400 B

Engine: 398 cc two cylinder overhead camshaft four-stroke, maximum output 36 bhp (DIN) at 8,500 rpm. Bore and stroke 64×62 mm. Compression ratio 9.5:1. Two 32 mm Keihin carburettors. Kick/electric start.
Transmission: primary drive by chain; final by chain. Six-speed gearbox. Wet multiplate clutch.
Ignition: battery and coil. 12v alternator.
Frame: tubular duplex cradle.
Suspension: front, telescopic forks; rear, swinging arm.
Tyres: front, 3.00×18; rear, 3.50×18.
Brakes: front, 231 mm disc; rear, 160 mm drum.
Tank capacity: 3.1 gallons (14 litres).
Weight: 374 lbs (170 kg).
Maximum speed: approximately 100 mph (160 kmh).

Manufacturer: Kawasaki Heavy Industries Ltd., Motorcycle Division, World Trade Centre Building, Tokyo.

KAWASAKI Z 650 B

Engine: 652 cc four cylinder double overhead camshaft four-stroke, maximum output 64 bhp (DIN) at 8,500 rpm. Bore and stroke 62×54 mm. Compression ratio 9.5:1. Four 24 mm Mikuni carburettors. Kick/electric start.
Transmission: primary drive by chain; final by chain. Five-speed gearbox. Wet multiplate clutch.
Ignition: battery and coil. 12v alternator.
Frame: tubular duplex cradle.
Suspension: front, telescopic forks; rear, swinging arm.
Tyres: front, 3.25×19; rear, 4.00×18.
Brakes: front, 250 mm disc; rear, 180 mm drum.
Tank capacity: 3.7 gallons (16.8 litres).
Weight: 487 lbs (211 kg).
Maximum speed: approximately 120 mph (193 kmh).

Manufacturer: Kawasaki Heavy Industries Ltd., Motorcycle Division, World Trade Centre Building, Tokyo.

KAWASAKI Z 750

Engine: 745 cc two cylinder four-stroke, maximum output 55 bhp (DIN) at 7,000 rpm. Bore and stroke 78×78 mm. Compression ratio 8.5:1. Two 38 mm Mikuni carburettors. Kick/electric start.
Transmission: primary drive by chain; final by chain. Five-speed gearbox. Wet multiplate clutch.
Ignition: battery and coil. 12v alternator.
Frame: tubular duplex cradle.
Suspension: front, telescopic forks; rear, swinging arm.
Tyres: front, 3.25×19; rear, 4.00×18.
Brakes: front, 245 mm disc; rear, 230 mm disc.
Tank capacity: 3.2 gallons (14.5 litres).
Weight: 481 lbs (218 kg).
Maximum speed: approximately 112 mph (180 kmh).

Manufacturer: Kawasaki Heavy Industries Ltd., Motorcycle Division, World Trade Centre Building, Tokyo.

KAWASAKI Z 1000 Z1 R

Engine: 1015 cc four cylinder double overhead camshaft four-stroke, maximum output 90 bhp (DIN) at 8,000 rpm. Bore and stroke 70×66 mm. Compression ratio 8.7:1. Four 28 mm Mikuni VM SS carburettors. Kick/electric start.
Transmission: primary drive by gears; final by self-lubricating chain. Five-speed gearbox. Wet multiplate clutch.
Ignition: battery and coil. 12v alternator.
Frame: tubular duplex cradle.
Suspension: front, telescopic forks; rear, swinging arm with adjustable shock absorbers.

Tyres: front, 3.50×18; rear, 4.00×18.
Brakes: front, 245 mm disc; rear, 250 mm disc.
Tank capacity: 3.8 gallons (17.6 litres).
Weight: 557 lbs (253 kg).
Maximum speed: approximately 129 mph (200 kmh).

Manufacturer: Kawasaki Heavy Industries Ltd., Motorcycle Division, World Trade Centre Building, Tokyo.

KAWASAKI Z 1000 ST

Engine: 1015 cc four cylinder double overhead camshaft four-stroke, maximum output 97 bhp (DIN) at 8,000 rpm. Bore and stroke 70×66 mm. Compression ratio 8.7:1. Four Mikuni 28 mm carburettors. Kick/electric start.
Transmission: primary drive by gears; final by shaft. Five-speed gearbox. Wet multiplate clutch.
Ignition: electronic.
Frame: tubular duplex cradle.
Suspension: front, telescopic forks; rear, swinging arm with adjustable shock absorbers.
Tyres: front, 3.25×19; rear, 4.50×17.

Brakes: front, 240 mm disc; rear, 250 mm disc.
Tank capacity: 3.9 gallons (17.6 litres).
Weight: 558 lbs (253 kg).
Maximum speed: approximately 124 mph (200 kmh).

Manufacturer: Kawasaki Heavy Industries Ltd., Motorcycle Division, World Trade Centre Building, Tokyo.

KAWASAKI Z 1300

Engine: 1286 cc six cylinder four-stroke, dohc water-cooled, maximum output 120 bhp (DIN) at 8,000 rpm. Bore and stroke 62×71 mm. Compression ratio 9.9:1. Three Mikuni BSW 32 carburettors. Electric/kick start.
Transmission: primary drive by gears; final by shaft. Five-speed gearbox. Wet multiplate clutch.
Ignition: electronic.
Frame: tubular duplex cradle.
Suspension: front, telescopic forks; rear, swinging arm and adjustable shock absorbers.
Tyres: front, 110/90×18; rear, 130/90×17.
Brakes: front, 260 mm discs; rear, 250 mm disc.
Tank capacity: 5.5 gallons (25 litres).
Weight: 639 lbs (290 kg).
Maximum speed: 130 mph (210 kmh).

Manufacturer: Kawasaki Heavy Industries Ltd., Motorcycle Division, World Trade Centre Building, Tokyo.

SUZUKI GT 125 C

Engine: 124 cc two cylinder two-stroke, maximum output 16 bhp (SAE) at 9,500 rpm. Bore and stroke 43×43 mm. Compression ratio 6.8:1. Two 18 mm Mikuni VM 18SC carburettors. Positive pump (CCI) lubrication. Kick start.
Transmission: primary drive by gears; final by chain. Five-speed gearbox. Wet multiplate clutch.
Ignition: battery and coil CDI.
Frame: tubular duplex cradle.
Suspension: front, telescopic forks; rear, swinging arm with adjustable shock absorbers.
Tyres: front, 2.75×18; rear, 3.00×18.

Brakes: front, 250 mm disc; rear, 130 mm drum.
Tank capacity: 2.2 gallons (10 litres).
Weight: 275 lbs (125 kg).
Maximum speed: approximately 74 mph (120 kmh).

Manufacturer: Suzuki Motor Co. Ltd., P.O. Box 116, Hamamatsu 430.

SUZUKI TS 250

Engine: 246 cc single cylinder two-stroke, maximum output 22 bhp (DIN) at 5,500 rpm. Bore and stroke 70×64 mm. Compression ratio 7:1. 28 mm Mikuni VM SS carburettor. Positive pump lubrication. Kick start.
Transmission: primary drive by gears; final by chain. Five-speed gearbox. Wet multiplate clutch.
Ignition: electronic.
Frame: tubular duplex cradle.
Suspension: front, telescopic forks; rear, swinging arm with adjustable shock absorbers.
Tyres: front, 3.00×21; rear, 4.00×18.

Brakes: front, 160 mm drum; rear, 160 mm drum.
Tank capacity: 2.2 gallons (10 litres).
Weight: 282 lbs (128 kg).
Maximum speed: approximately 75 mph (120 kmh).

Manufacturer: Suzuki Motor Co. Ltd., P.O. Box 116, Hamamatsu 430.

SUZUKI GS 550 EN

Engine: 549 cc four cylinder double overhead camshaft four-stroke, maximum output 51 bhp (DIN) at 7,500 rpm. Bore and stroke 56×55.8 mm. Compression ratio 8.6:1. Four 22 mm Mikuni VM 22SS carburettors. Wet sump lubrication. Kick/electric start.
Transmission: primary drive by gears; final by chain. Six-speed gearbox. Wet multiplate clutch.
Ignition: battery and coil 12v/196w alternator.
Frame: tubular duplex cradle.
Suspension: front, telescopic forks; rear, swinging arm with adjustable shock absorbers.

Tyres: front, 3.25 × 19; rear, 3.75 × 18.
Brakes front, 275 mm disc; rear, 275 mm disc.
Tank capacity: 3.7 gallons (16.8 litres).
Weight: 461 lbs (209 kg).
Maximum speed: approximately 115 mph (185 kmh).

Manufacturer: Suzuki Motor Co. Ltd., P.O. Box 116, Hamamatsu 430.

SUZUKI GT 750

Engine: 738 cc three cylinder two-stroke with water cooling system, maximum output 65.4 bhp (DIN) at 6,500 rpm. Bore and stroke 70×64 mm. Compression ratio 6.7:1. Three BS carburettors with 40 mm choke. Oil injection lubrication. Electric/kick start.
Transmission: primary drive by gears; final by chain. Five-speed gearbox. Wet multiplate clutch.
Ignition: coil. 12v/250w alternator.
Frame: tubular duplex cradle.
Suspension: front, telescopic forks; rear, swinging arm and adjustable shock absorbers.

Tyres: front, 3.25×19; rear, 4.00×19.
Brakes: front, 295 mm discs; rear, 180 mm drum.
Tank capacity: 4 gallons (17 litres).
Weight: 507 lbs (230 kg).
Maximum speed: 124 mph (200 kmh).

Manufacturer: Suzuki Motor Co. Ltd., P.O. Box 116, Hamamatsu 430.

SUZUKI EN 750

Engine: 748 cc four cylinder double overhead camshaft four-stroke, maximum output 68 bhp at 8,500 rpm. Bore and stroke 65 × 56.4 mm. Compression ratio 8.7:1. Four 26 mm Mikuni VM 26SS carburettors. Wet sump lubrication. Kick/electric start.
Transmission: primary drive by gears; final by chain. Five-speed gearbox. Wet multiplate clutch.
Ignition: battery and coil 12v/196w alternator.
Frame: tubular duplex cradle.
Suspension: front, telescopic forks; rear, swinging arm with adjustable shock absorbers.
Tyres: front, 3.25 × 19; rear, 4.00 × 18.
Brakes: front, 275 mm disc; rear, 275 mm disc.
Tank capacity: 4 gallons (18 litres).
Weight: 491 lbs (223 kg).
Maximum speed: approximately 125 mph (200 kmh).

Manufacturer: Suzuki Motor Co. Ltd., P.O. Box 116, Hamamatsu 430.

SUZUKI GS 850

Engine: 843 cc four cylinder four-stroke, dohc, maximum output 78 bhp (DIN) at 9000 rpm. Bore and stroke 69 × 56.4 mm. Compression ratio 8.8:1. Four Mikuni VM 26 SS carburettors. Wet sump lubrication.
Transmission: primary drive by gears; final by shaft. Five-speed gearbox. Wet multiplate clutch.
Ignition: electronic.
Frame: tubular duplex cradle.
Suspension: front, telescopic fork; rear, swinging arm with adjustable shock absorbers.
Tyres: front, 3.50 × 19; rear, 4.50 × 17.
Brakes: front, disc; rear, disc.
Tank capacity: 5 gallons (22 litres).
Weight: 558 lbs (253 kg).
Maximum speed: 126 mph (206 kmh).

Manufacturer: Suzuki Motor Co. Ltd., P.O. Box 116, Hamamatsu 430.

SUZUKI GS 1000

Engine: 993 cc four cylinder double overhead camshaft four-stroke, maximum output 87 bhp at 8,000 rpm. Bore and stroke 70 × 64.8 mm. Compression ratio 9.2:1. Four 26 mm Mikuni VM 26SS carburettors. Wet sump lubrication. Electric start.
Transmission: primary drive by gears; final by chain. Five-speed gearbox. Wet multiplate clutch.
Ignition: battery and coil 12v/200w alternator.
Frame: tubular duplex cradle.
Suspension: front, telescopic forks; rear, swinging arm with adjustable shock absorbers.
Tyres: front, 3.25 × 19; rear, 4.50 × 17.
Brakes front, two 295 mm discs; rear, 295 mm disc.
Tank capacity: 4.00 gallons (18 litres).
Weight: 516 lbs (234 kg).
Maximum speed: approximately 139 mph (223 kmh).

Manufacturer: Suzuki Motor Co. Ltd., P.O. Box 116, Hamamatsu 430.

YAMAHA DT 50 M

Engine: 49 cc single cylinder two-stroke, maximum output 1.9 bhp (DIN) at 5,500 rpm. Bore and stroke 40 × 39.7 mm. Compression ratio 6.8:1. Positive pump. Kick start.
Transmission: primary drive by gears; final by chain. Five-speed gearbox. Wet multiplate clutch.
Ignition: flywheel magneto.
Frame: tubular duplex.
Suspension: front, telescopic forks; rear, swinging arm with adjustable shock absorbers.
Tyres: front, 2.50 × 19; rear, 3.00 × 17.
Brakes: front, drum; rear, drum.

Tank capacity: 1 gallon (6 litres).
Weight: 163 lbs (74 kg).
Maximum speed: not stated.

Manufacturer: Yamaha Motor Co. Ltd., 1280 Nakajo, Hamakita-Shi, Shizuoka-Ken.

YAMAHA RD 50 M

Engine: 49 cc single cylinder two-stroke, maximum output 3 bhp (DIN) at 5,000 rpm. Bore and stroke 40 × 39.7 mm. Compression ratio 6.8:1. Kick start.
Transmission: primary drive by gears; final by chain. Five-speed gearbox. Wet multiplate clutch.
Ignition: flywheel magneto. 6v.
Frame: tubular duplex cradle.
Suspension: front, telescopic forks; rear, swinging arm.
Tyres: front, 2.50 × 18; rear, 3.00 × 18.
Brakes: front, 205 mm disc; rear, drum.

Tank capacity: 1.76 gallons (8 litres).
Weight: 178 lbs (81 kg).
Maximum speed: not stated.

Manufacturer: Yamaha Motor Co. Ltd., 1280 Nakajo, Hamakita-Shi, Shizuoka-Ken.

YAMAHA FSI-DX

Engine: 49 cc single cylinder two-stroke, maximum output 2.6 bhp (DIN) at 5,000 rpm. Bore and stroke 40 × 39.7 mm. Compression ratio 7.1:1. Kick start.
Transmission: primary drive by gears; final by chain. Four-speed gearbox. Wet multiplate clutch.
Ignition: flywheel magneto 6v.
Frame: reinforced pressed steel.
Suspension: front, telescopic forks; rear, swinging arm.
Tyres: front, 2.50 × 17; rear, 2.50 × 17.
Brakes: front, 203 mm disc; rear, drum.

Tank capacity: 1.4 gallons (6.5 litres).
Weight: 156 lbs. (71 kg).
Maximum speed: approximately 50 mph (80 kmh).

Manufacturer: Yamaha Motor Co. Ltd., 1280 Nakajo, Hamakita-Shi, Shizuoka-Ken.

YAMAHA DT 125 E

Engine: 123 cc single cylinder two-stroke, maximum output 13 bhp (DIN) at 7,000 rpm. Bore and stroke 56×50 mm. Compression ratio 7.1:1. Kick/electric start.
Transmission: primary drive by gears; final by chain. Five-speed gearbox. Wet multiplate clutch.
Ignition: battery and coil. 6v.
Frame: tubular duplex cradle.
Suspension: front, telescopic forks; rear, swinging arm.
Tyres: front, 2.75×21; rear, 3.25×18.
Brakes: front, drum; rear, drum.
Tank capacity: 1.76 gallons (8 litres).

Weight: 230.42 lbs (104.5 kg).
Maximum speed: not stated.

Manufacturer: Yamaha Motor Co. Ltd., 1280 Nakajo, Hamakita-Shi, Shizuoka-Ken.

YAMAHA YZ 125

Engine: 123 cc single cylinder two-stroke, maximum output 26 bhp (DIN) at 11,000 rpm. Bore and stroke 50×50 mm. Compression ratio 8.3:1. Mikuni 34 carburettor. Kick start.
Transmission: primary drive by gears; final by chain. Six-speed gearbox. Wet multiplate clutch.
Ignition: electronic.
Frame: tubular duplex cradle.
Suspension: front, telescopic fork; rear, monocross.
Tyres: front, 3.00×21; rear, 4.10×18.
Brakes: drum.

Tank capacity: 1.3 gallons (6.1 litres).
Weight: 194 lbs (88 kg).
Maximum speed: not stated.

Manufacturer: Yamaha Motor Co. Ltd., 1280 Nakajo, Hamakita-Shi, Shizuoka-Ken.

YAMAHA YZ 250

Engine: 246 cc single cylinder two-stroke, maximum output 37 bhp (DIN) at 7,500 rpm. Bore and stroke 70×64 mm. Compression ratio 7.8:1. Mikuni 34 carburettor. Kick start.
Transmission: primary drive by gears; final by chain. Six-speed pedal-operated gearbox. Wet multiplate clutch.
Ignition: electronic.
Frame: tubular duplex cradle.
Suspension: front, adjustable telefork; rear, monocross.
Tyres: front, 3.00×21; rear, 4.50×18.
Brakes: drum front and rear.

Tank capacity: 1.7 gallons (7.6 litres).
Weight: 218 lbs (99 kg).
Maximum speed: not stated.

Manufacturer: Yamaha Motor Co. Ltd., 1280 Nakajo, Hamakita-Shi, Shizuoka-Ken.

YAMAHA XS 1100

Engine: 1100 cc four cylinder double overhead camshaft four-stroke, maximum output 95 bhp (DIN) at 8,000 rpm. Bore and stroke 71.5 × 68.6 mm. Compression ratio 9.2:1. Four 34 Mikuni VM SS carburettors. Pressure-fed wet sump lubrication. Kick/electric start.
Transmission: primary drive by chain and gears; final by shaft. Five-speed gearbox. Wet multiplate clutch.
Ignition: electronic.
Frame: tubular duplex cradle.
Suspension: front, telescopic forks; rear, swinging arm with adjustable shock absorbers.
Tyres: front, 3.50 × 19; rear, 4.50 × 17.
Brakes: front, 298 mm discs; rear, 298 mm disc.
Tank capacity: 5.25 gallons (24 litres).
Weight: 563 lbs (256 kg).
Maximum speed: approximately 136 mph (220 kmh).

Manufacturer: Yamaha Motor Co. Ltd., 1280 Nakajo, Hamakita-Shi, Shizuoka-Ken.

BATAVUS STARFLITE GTS

Engine: 49 cc single cylinder two-stroke, maximum output 6.25 bhp (DIN) at 8,000 rpm. Bore and stroke 38×44 mm. Compression ratio 10:1. 19 mm Bing carburettor. 24:1 petroil lubrication. Kick start.
Transmission: primary drive by gears; final by chain. Five-speed gearbox. Wet multiplate clutch.
Ignition: Motoplat Thyristor flywheel magneto. 6v.
Frame: tubular duplex cradle.
Suspension: front, telescopic forks; rear, swinging arm.
Tyres: front, 2.75×17; rear, 2.75×17.
Brakes: front, 160 mm drum; rear, 125 mm drum.
Tank capacity: 2.5 gallons (11 litres).
Weight: 178 lbs (81 kg).
Maximum speed: approximately 56 mph (90 kmh).

Manufacturer: Batavus Intercycle B.V., Heerenveen, Industrieweg 4.

WSK GIL 125

Engine: 125cc single cylinder two-stroke, maximum output 7.3 bhp (DIN) at 5,300 rpm. Bore and stroke 52×58 mm. Compression ratio 7.8:1. 24 mm carburettor. Petroil lubrication. Kick start.
Transmission: primary and final drive by chain. Wet multiplate clutch.
Ignition: 6V 25W magneto flywheel.
Frame: single tubular cradle.
Suspension: front, telescopic forks; rear, swinging arm.
Tyres: front, 3.00×18; rear, 3.00×18.
Brakes: front, 135 mm drum; rear, 135 mm drum.

Tank capacity: 1.9 gallons (8.5 litres).
Weight: 214 lbs (97 kg).
Maximum speed: approximately 50 mph (80 kmh).

Manufacturer: WSK "PZL-Swidnik", 21-045 Swidnik, PHZ Pezetel 00-950 Warsaw POB No. 371.

WSK KOBUZ 175

Engine: 175cc single-cylinder two-stroke, maximum output 14 bhp (DIN) at 6,000 rpm. Bore and stroke 61×59.5 mm. Compression ratio 9:1. 26 mm carburettor. Petroil lubrication. Kick start.
Transmission: primary and final drive by chain. Four-speed gearbox. Wet multiplate clutch.
Ignition: 6V 35W magneto flywheel.
Frame: single cradle.
Suspension: front, telescopic forks; rear, swinging arm.
Tyres: front, 3.00×18; rear, 3.00×18.

Brakes: front, 135 mm drum; rear, 135 mm drum.
Tank capacity: 1.9 galls (8.5 litres).
Weight: 247 lbs (112 kg).
Maximum speed: 65 mph (105 kmh).

Manufacturer: WSK "PZL-Swidnik", 21-045 Swidnik, PHZ Pezetel 00-950 Warsaw POB No. 371.

CASAL K 182

Engine: 49.8 cc single cylinder two-stroke, maximum output 5.3 bhp at 7,500 rpm. Bore and stroke 40 × 39.7 mm. Compression ratio 8.5:1. 9 mm Bing carburettor. 33:1 petroil lubrication. Kick start.
Transmission: primary drive by gears; final by chain. Four-speed gearbox. Wet multiplate clutch.
Ignition: flywheel magneto.
Frame: tubular single beam.
Suspension: front, telescopic forks; rear, swinging arm.
Tyres: front, 2.75 × 21; rear, 2.75 × 17.
Brakes front, 140 mm drum; rear, 140 mm drum.
Tank capacity: 2.6 gallons (12 litres).
Weight: 161 lbs (73 kg).

Maximum speed: approximately 50 mph (80 kmh).

Manufacturer: Metalurgia Casal SARL, Apartado 82, Aveiro.

CASAL K 190

Engine: 49.8 cc single cylinder two-stroke, maximum output 5.3bhp (DIN) at 8,500 rpm. Bore and stroke 40 × 39.7 mm. Compression ratio 8.5:1. 16 mm Mikuni carburettor. 33:1 petroil lubrication. Kick start.
Transmission: primary drive by gears; final by chain. Four-speed gearbox. Wet multiplate clutch.
Ignition: flywheel magneto 6v.
Frame: tubular single beam.
Suspension: front, telescopic forks; rear, swinging arm.
Tyres: front, 2.75 × 21; rear, 2.75 × 17.
Brakes: front, 140 mm drum; rear, 140 mm drum.
Tank capacity: 1.7 gallons (8 litres).
Weight: 159 lbs (72 kg).
Maximum speed: approximately 50 mph (80 kmh).

Manufacturer: Metalurgia Casal SARL, Apartado 83, Aveiro.

BULTACO STREAKER 74/125

Engine: 74.7 (118.82) cc single cylinder two-stroke, maximum output 6.5 (8.9) bhp (DIN) at 8,500 (9,000) rpm. Bore and stroke 43 (54.2) × 51.5 mm. Compression ratio 12.5 (12):1. 22 mm Amal 2600 (26 mm Bing 84) carburettor. 19:1 petroil lubrication. Kick start.
Transmission: primary drive by chain; final by chain. Six-speed gearbox.
Ignition: flywheel magneto, 6v alternator.
Frame: tubular duplex cradle.
Suspension: front, telescopic forks; rear, swinging arm with adjustable shock absorbers.
Tyres: front, 2.50 × 18; rear, 2.75 × 18.
Brakes front, 220 mm disc; rear, 220 mm disc.
Tank capacity: 2.3 gallons (10.5 litres).
Weight: 187 lbs (85 kg).
Maximum speed: not stated.

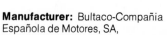

Manufacturer: Bultaco-Campañia Española de Motores, SA, Barcelona.

BULTACO FRONTERA 74

Engine: 74.7 cc single cylinder two-stroke, maximum output 10.5 bhp (DIN) at 8,000 rpm. Bore and stroke 43×51.5 mm. Compression ratio 10.5:1. Amal 25 mm carburettor. Petroil lubrication. Kick start.
Transmission: primary and final by chain. Six-speed gear-box. Wet multiplate clutch.
Ignition: magneto flywheel with Duplex chain.
Frame: single beam split underneath.
Suspension: front, telescopic forks; rear, swinging arm.

Tyres: front, 2.75×21; rear, 3.50×18.
Brakes: front, 125 mm drum; rear, 125 mm drum.
Tank capacity: 1.2 gallons (5.5 litres).
Weight: 191 lbs (86.5 kg).
Maximum speed: not stated.

Manufacturer: Bultaco Compañia Española de Motores, SA, Barcelona.

BULTACO MERCURIO 175 GT

Engine: 176 cc single cylinder two-stroke, maximum output 12.49 bhp at 6,000 rpm. Bore and stroke 61.5 × 60 mm. Compression ratio 7.5:1. 22 mm Zenith carburettor. 19:1 petroil lubrication. Kick start.
Transmission: primary drive by duplex chain; final by fully-enclosed chain. Five-speed gearbox. Wet multiplate clutch.
Ignition: flywheel magneto, 6v/40w.
Frame: tubular duplex cradle.
Suspension: front, telescopic forks; rear, swinging arm.
Tyres: front, 3.00 × 17; rear, 3.00 × 17.

Brakes: front, 140 mm drum; rear, 140 mm drum.
Tank capacity: 2.6 gallons (11.5 litres).
Weight: 209 lbs (95 kg).
Maximum speed: approximately 69 mph (112 kmh).

Manufacturer: Bultaco-Compañia Española de Motores, SA, Barcelona.

BULTACO METRALLA GTS 250

Engine: 244 cc single cylinder two-stroke, maximum output 25 bhp (DIN) at 7,500 rpm. Bore and stroke 72 × 60 mm. Compression ratio 10:1. Bing 84 carburettor. 19:1 petroil lubrication.
Transmission: primary drive by chain; final by fully-enclosed chain. Six-speed gearbox. Wet multiplate clutch.
Ignition: electronic.
Frame: tubular cradle.
Suspension: front, telescopic forks; rear, swinging arm.
Tyres: front, 3.00 × 18; rear, 3.25 × 18.

Brakes: front, 160 mm drum; rear, 160 mm drum.
Tank capacity: 2,9 gallons (13 litres).
Weight: 266 lbs (121 kg).
Maximum speed: approximately 93 mph (150 kmh).

Manufacturer: Bultaco-Campania Española de Motores, SA, Barcelona.

BULTACO ALPINA 250

Engine: 237.45 cc single cylinder two-stroke, maximum output 14.1 bhp (DIN) at 5,500 rpm. Bore and stroke 71 × 60 mm. Compression ratio 9:1. Amal 27 carburettor. 19:1 petroil lubrication. Kick start.
Transmission: primary drive by duplex chain; final by chain. Five-speed gearbox. Wet multiplate clutch.
Ignition: flywheel magneto 6v/40w.
Frame: tubular duplex cradle.
Suspension: front, telescopic forks; rear, swinging arm.
Tyres: front, 2.75 × 21; rear, 4.00 × 18.

Brakes: front, 140 mm drum; rear, 140 mm drum.
Tank Capacity: 1.9 gallons (8.5 litres).
Weight: 232 lbs (105 kg).
Maximum speed: not stated.

Manufacturer: Bultaco-Campañia Española de Motores, SA, Barcelona.

BULTACO PURSANG MK 12 250/370

Engine: 246.3 (363.2) cc single cylinder two-stroke, maximum output 38.8 (42.2) bhp (DIN) at 8,700 (8000) rpm. Bore and stroke 70×64 (85×64) mm. Compression ratio 11:1 (10:1). Bing 54/2 38 mm carburettor. Kick start.
Transmission: primary and final drive by unenclosed chain. Five-speed gearbox. Wet multiple clutch.
Ignition: electronic.
Frame: tubular duplex cradle.
Suspension: front, telefork; rear, swinging arm.
Tyres: front, 3.00×21; rear, 4.50×18.

Brakes: front, 125 (140) mm drum; rear, 140 mm drum.
Tank capacity: 2.3 gallons (10.5 litres).
Weight: 218 (225) lbs (99 [102] kg).
Maximum speed: not stated.

Manufacturer: Bultaco-Campañia Española de Motores, SA, Barcelona.

BULTACO SHERPA T 250

Engine: 237.5 cc single cylinder two-stroke, maximum output 14.14 bhp (DIN) at 5,500 rpm. Bore and stroke 71 × 60 mm. Compression ratio 9:1. 27 mm Amal carburettor. 19:1 petroil lubrication. Kick start.
Transmission: primary drive by chain; final by chain. Five-speed gearbox. Wet multiplate clutch.
Ignition: flywheel magneto 6v/40w.
Frame: tubular duplex single beam.
Suspension: front, telescopic forks; rear, swinging arm.

Tyres: front, 2.75 × 21; rear, 4.00 × 18.
Brakes: front, 125 mm drum; rear, 125 mm drum.
Tank capacity: 1.1 gallons (5 litres).
Weight: 204 lbs (92.5 kg).
Maximum speed: not stated.

Manufacturer: Bultaco-Compañia Española de Motores, SA, Barcelona.

BULTACO FRONTERA Mk II 250/370

Engine: 246.3 (363.1) cc single cylinder two-stroke, maximum output 37 (42.2) bhp (DIN) at 8,720 (7,500) rpm. Bore and stroke 70×64 (85×64) mm. Compression ratio 11:1 (10:1). Amal 2000 38 mm carburettor. Petrol lubrication. Kick start.
Transmission: primary and final drive by chain. Six- (five)-speed gearbox. Wet multiplate clutch.
Ignition: motoplat.
Frame: single cradle split under the engine.
Suspension: front, telefork; rear, swinging arm.
Tyres: front, 3.00×21; rear, 4.50×18.
Brakes: front 140 mm drum; rear 30 mm. drum.
Tank capacity: 2.3 gallons (10.5 litres).
Weight: 236 (240) lbs (107 [109] kg).
Maximum speed: not stated.

Manufacturer: Bultaco-Campañia Española de Motorers, SA, Barcelona.

MONTESA COTA 348

Engine: 305.8 cc single cylinder two-stroke, maximum output and compression ratio not stated. Bore and stroke 78×64 mm. 27 mm carburettor. Petroil lubrication.
Transmission: primary drive by gears; final by chain.
Ignition: flywheel magneto.
Frame: tubular duplex cradle.
Suspension: front, teleforks; rear, swinging arm.
Tyres: front, 2.75×21; rear, 4.00×18.
Brakes: front 110 mm; rear 110 mm drum.
Tank capacity: 1.1 gallons (5 litres).

Weight: 196 lbs (89 kg).
Maximum speed: not stated.

Manufacturer: Motocicletas Montesa SA, Virgeen Paloma 21, Esplugas, Barcelona.

MONTESA COTA 348 TRIAL

Engine: 306 cc single cylinder two-stroke, maximum output 16 bhp (DIN) at 5,500 rpm. Bore and stroke 78 × 64 mm. Compression ratio 9:1. 27 mm carburettor. 24:1 petroil lubrication. Kick start.
Transmission: primary drive by gears; final by chain. Six-speed gearbox. Wet multiplate clutch.
Ignition: flywheel magneto.
Frame: tubular duplex cradle.
Suspension: front, telescopic forks; rear, swinging arm.
Tyres: front, 2.75 × 21; rear, 4.00 × 18.
Brakes: front, 110 mm drum; rear, 110 mm drum.

Tank capacity: 1.1 gallons (5 litres).
Weight: 196 lbs (89 kg).
Maximum speed: not stated.

Manufacturer: Motocicletas Montesa SA, Virgeen Paloma 21, Esplugas, Barcelona.

MONTESA CAPPRA 414 VE

Engine: 413.5 cc single cylinder two-stroke. Compression ratio and maximum output not stated. Bore and stroke not stated. Bing 40 mm carburettor. Petroil lubrication. Kick start.
Transmission: primary drive by gears; final by chain. Four-speed gearbox. Wet multiplate clutch.
Ignition: electronic magneto flywheel.
Frame: duplex cradle.
Suspension: front, telefork; rear, swinging arm.
Tyres: front, 3.00×21; rear, 5.00×17.
Brakes: front, 130 mm drum; rear,

150 mm conical drum expansion brakes.
Tank capacity: 1.9 gallons (8.4 litres).
Weight: 218 lbs (99 kg).
Maximum speed: not stated.

Manufacturer: Motocicletas Montessa SA, Virgeen Paloma 21, Esplugas, Barcelona.

MOTOTRANS-DUCATI MINI 3

Engine: 47.6 cc single cylinder two-stroke. Compression ratio and maximum output not stated. Bore and stroke 38×42 mm. Amal carburettor with 12 mm choke. Petroil lubrication. Kick start.
Transmission: primary drive by gears; final by chain. Three-speed gearbox. Wet multiplate clutch.
Ignition: Motoplat electronic flywheel.
Frame: single cradle.
Suspension: front, telefork; rear, swinging arm.
Tyres: front, 3.00×12; rear, 3.00×12.
Brakes: 100 mm drum.

Tank capacity: 1.16 gallons (5.3 litres).
Weight: 143 lbs (65 kg).
Maximum speed: not stated.

Manufacturer: Maquinaria y Elementos de Transporte S A (Mototrans), Almogalvares 181, Barcelona.

MOTOTRANS-DUCATI 350 VENTO

Engine: 340.2 cc single cylinder four-stroke, maximum output 28 bhp (DIN) at 7,500 rpm. Bore and stroke 76 × 75 mm. Compression ratio 10:1. 32 mm Dell'Orto PHF carburettor. Kick start.
Transmission: primary drive by gears; final by chain. Five-speed gearbox. Wet multiplate clutch.
Ignition: flywheel 6v/60w alternator.
Frame: tubular cradle.
Suspension: front, telescopic forks; rear, swinging arm with gas shock absorbers.
Tyres: front, 3.25 × 18; rear, 3.50 × 18.
Brakes: front, 230 mm discs; rear, 260 mm disc.
Tank capacity: 3.5 gallons (16 litres).
Weight: 308 lbs (140 kg).
Maximum speed: approximately 104 mph (168 kmh).

Manufacturer: Maquinaria y Elementos De Transporte SA (Mototrans), Almogalvares 181, Barcelona.

MOTOTRANS DUCATI 500 DESMO

Engine: 496.9 cc two cylinder four-stroke with parallel cylinders, dohc, maximum output 45 bhp (DIN) at 7,250 rpm. Bore and stroke 78×52 mm. Compression ratio 9.6:1. Two Dell'Orto PHF 30 mm DB/BS carburettors. Sump lubrication. Electric start.
Transmission: primary drive by gears; final by chain. Five-speed gearbox. Wet multiplate clutch.
Ignition: PT Motoplat alternator, 12v 18Ah battery.
Frame: open tubular cradle.
Suspension: front, telescopic fork; rear, swinging arm with adjustable shock absorbers.
Tyres: front, 3.25×18 Racing; rear, 3.50×18.
Brakes: front, 260 mm hydraulic discs; rear, 260 mm disc.
Tank capacity: 3 gallons (14 litres).
Weight: 392 lbs (178 kg).
Maximum speed: 112 mph (180 kmh).

Manufacturer: Maquinaria y Elementos de Transporte S.A. (Mototrans), Almogalvares 181, Barcelona.

OSSA 250 TURISMO

Engine: 250 cc single cylinder two-stroke, maximum output not stated. Bore and stroke 60×72 mm. Compression ratio 12:1. 32 mm Amal carburettor. 19:1 petroil lubrication. Kick start.
Transmission: primary drive by gears; final by chain. Five-speed gearbox. Wet multiplate clutch.
Ignition: Motoplat flywheel magneto 6v.
Frame: tubular duplex cradle.
Suspension: front, telescopic forks; rear, swinging arm.
Tyres: front, 3.00×19; rear, 3.25×18.
Brakes: front, 163 mm drum; rear, 163 mm drum.
Tank capacity: 2.9 gallons (13.25 litres).
Weight: 236 lbs (107 kg).
Maximum speed: approximately 87 mph (140 kmh).

Manufacturer: Maquinaria Cinematografica SA, (Ossa Motor cycles), Poligno Industrial Zona Franca, Barcelona.

OSSA 500 YANKEE

Engine: 488 cc two cylinder two-stroke, maximum output 58 bhp (DIN) at 7,500 rpm. Bore and stroke 72×60 mm. Compression ratio 8:1. 32 mm Bing carburettor. Kick start.
Transmission: primary drive by chain; final by chain. Six-speed gearbox. Wet multiplate clutch.
Ignition: Motoplat magneto 6v.
Frame: tubular duplex cradle.
Suspension: front, telescopic forks; rear, swinging arm with gas shock absorbers.
Tyres: front, 3.25×19; rear, 4.00×18.
Brakes: front, disc; rear, disc.
Tank capacity: 4 gallons (18 litres).
Weight: 348 lbs (158 kg).
Maximum speed: approximately 115 mph (185 kmh).

Manufacturer: Maquinaria Cinematografica SA, (Ossa Motor cycles), Poligno Industrial Zona Franca, Barcelona.

SANGLAS 500 S

Engine: 496 cc single cylinder four-stroke, maximum output 32 bhp (DIN) at 6,700 rpm. Bore and stroke 89.5×79 mm. Compression ratio 8:1. 30 mm Amal carburettor. Electric start.
Transmission: primary drive by duplex chain; final by chain. Four-speed gearbox. Wet multiplate clutch.
Ignition: Femsa battery and coil. 12v/110w.
Frame: tubular duplex cradle.
Suspension: front telescopic froks; rear, swinging arm.
Tyres: front, 3.25×18; rear, 3.50×18.
Brakes: front, 180 mm drum; rear, 180 mm drum.
Tank capacity: 3.3 gallons (15 litres).
Weight: 388 lbs (176 kg).

Maximum speed: approximately 100 mph (160 kmh).

Manufacturer: Sanglas SA, Rambla Justo Oliveras SN, Hospitalet, Barcelona.

SACHS 125/175 GS

Engine: 123 (171) cc single cylinder two-stroke, maximum output 245 (300) bhp (DIN) at 8,700 (9,600) rpm. Bore and stroke 53.75×54 mm. Compression ratio 12 (11.5):1. 32 (34) mm Bing carburettor. Petroil lubrication. Kick start.
Transmission: primary drive by gears; final drive by chain. Seven-speed gearbox. Wet multiplate clutch.
Ignition: electronic.
Frame: tubular duplex cradle.
Suspension: front, telescopic forks; rear, swinging arm with adjustable shock absorbers.

Tyres: front, 3.00×21; rear, 4.00 (4.50) ×18.
Brakes: 140 mm conical drum.
Tank capacity: 2 gallons (9.5 litres).
Weight: 203 (214) lbs (92 [97] kg).
Maximum speed: not stated.

Manufacturer: Sachs AG, Postfach 1140, 8720 Schweinfurt.

SACHS 175(250) GS

Engine: 171 (255.3) cc single cylinder two-stroke, maximum output 30 (36) bhp (DIN) at 8,700 (8,300) rpm. Bore and stroke 59.7 (73)×61 mm. Compression ratio 11.5:1. 34 (36) mm Bing carburettor. 49:1 petroil lubrication. Kick start.
Transmission: primary drive by gears; final by chain. Seven-speed gearbox. Wet multiplate clutch.
Ignition: Motoplat electronic.
Frame: duplex cradle.
Suspension: front, telescopic forks; rear, swinging arm with gas shock absorbers.

Tyres: front, 3.00×21; rear, 4.50×18.
Brakes: front, 140 mm drum; rear, 140 mm drum.
Tank capacity: 2.1 gallons (9.5 litres).
Weight: 213 (222) lbs (96.6 [100.6] kg).
Maximum speed: not stated.

Manufacturer: Sachs AG, Postfach 1140, 8720 Schweinfurt.

SACHS 250 CROSS

Engine: 248.4 cc single cylinder two-stroke, maximum output 35 bhp at 7,800 rpm. Bore and stroke 72×61 mm. Compression ratio 11.5:1. Bing carburettor with 38 mm choke. Kick start.
Transmission: primary drive by gears; final by chain. Five-speed gearbox. Wet multiplate clutch.
Ignition: electronic.
Frame: tubular duplex cradle.
Suspension: front, telescopic forks; rear, swinging arm with adjustable shock absorbers.
Tyres: front, 3.00×21; rear, 4.50×18.

Brakes: front, 140 mm conical drum; rear, 160 mm conical drum.
Tank capacity: 1.9 gallons (8.5 litres).
Weight: 209 lbs (95 kg).
Maximum speed: not stated.

Manufacturer: Sachs AG, Postfach 1140, 8720 Schweinfurt.

SACHS 250/350 GS

Engine: 245 (255.3) cc single cylinder four-stroke, maximum output 37 bhp (DIN) at 8,300 rpm. Bore and stroke 71.5 (73)×61 mm. Compression ratio 11.5:1. Bing 36 carburettor. Petroil lubrication. Kick start.
Transmission: primary drive by gears; final by chain. Seven-speed gearbox. Wet multiplate clutch.
Ignition: electronic.
Frame: tubular duplex cradle.
Suspension: front, telescopic forks; rear, swinging arm with adjustable shock absorbers.

Tyres: front, 3.00×21; rear 4.50×18.
Brakes: 140 mm conical drum.
Tank capacity: 2 gallons (9.5 litres).
Weight: 223 lbs (101 kg).
Maximum speed: not stated.

Manufacturer: Sachs AG, Postfach 1140, 8720 Schweinfurt.

ZÜNDAPP GTS 50

Engine: 49.9 cc single cylinder two-stroke, maximum output 2.9 bhp (DIN) at 4,900 rpm. Bore and stroke 39×41.8 mm. Compression ratio 9:1. 19 mm Bing carburettor. 24:1 petroil lubrication. Kick start.
Transmission: primary drive by gears; final by chain. Four-speed gearbox. Wet multiplate clutch.
Ignition: Bosch Thyristor. 6v.
Frame: pressed steel tubular.
Suspension: front, telescopic forks; rear, swinging arm.
Tyres: front, 2.75×21; rear, 2.75×21.

Brakes: front, 155 mm drum; rear, 155 mm drum.
Tank capacity: 3 gallons (13.5 litres).
Weight: 190 lbs (86 kg).
Maximum speed: approximately 25 mph (40 kmh).

Manufacturer: Zündapp-Werke GmbH, 8 München 80, Anzinger Strasse, 1–3.

ZÜNDAPP KS 50 TT

Engine: 49 cc single cylinder water-cooled two-stroke, maximum output 6.8 bhp (DIN) at 8,800 rpm. Bore and stroke 39×41.8 mm. Compression ratio 11:1. 20 mm Mikuni carburettor. 24:1 petroil lubrication. Kick start.
Transmission: primary drive by gears; final by chain. Five-speed gearbox. Wet multiplate clutch.
Ignition: electronic 6v.
Frame: pressed steel tubular cradle.
Suspension: front, telescopic forks; rear, swinging arm.

Tyres: front, 2.75×21; rear, 2.75×21.
Brakes: front, 220 mm disc; rear, 150 mm drum.
Tank capacity: 3 gallons (13.5 litres).
Weight: 208 lbs (94 kg).
Maximum speed: approximately 53 mph (85 kmh).

Manufacturer: Zündapp-Werke GmbH, 8 München 80, Anzinger Strasse, 1–3.

ZÜNDAPP KS 50 SUPER SPORT TT

Engine: 49.9 cc single cylinder two-stroke, maximum output 67 bhp (DIN) at 8,800 rpm. Bore and stroke 39×41.8 mm. Compression ratio 11:1. Mikuni 19 mm carburettor. Petroil lubrication. Kick start.
Transmission: primary drive by gears; final by chain. Five-speed gearbox. Wet multiplate clutch.
Ignition: electronic.
Frame: tubular duplex cradle.
Suspension: front, telescopic forks; rear, swinging arm.
Tyres: 2.75×17.
Brakes: front, 220 mm disc; rear, 150 mm drum.

Tank capacity: 3 gallons (13.5 litres).
Weight: 209 lbs (95 kg).
Maximum speed: 52 mph (85 kmh).

Manufacturer: Zündapp-Werke GmbH, 8 München 80, Anziger Str. 1-3.

ZÜNDAPP GS 125

Engine: 123 cc single cylinder two-stroke, maximum output 21 bhp (DIN) at 8,500 rpm. Bore and stroke 54×54 mm. Compression ratio 11.3:1. 28 mm Bing carburettor. 50:1 petroil lubrication. Kick start.
Transmission: primary drive by gears; final by chain. Five-speed gearbox. Wet multiplate clutch.
Ignition: Bosch Thyristor. 6v.
Frame: tubular duplex cradle.
Suspension: front, telescopic forks; rear, swinging arm.
Tyres: front, 3.00×21; rear, 3.75×18.

Brakes: front, 150 mm drum; rear, 150 mm drum.
Tank capacity: 1.6 gallons (7.28 litres).
Weight: 187 lbs (84.82kg).
Maximum speed: not stated.

Manufacturer: Zündapp-Werke GmbH, 8 München 80, Anzinger Strasse, 1–3.

ZÜNDAPP KS 175

Engine: 163 cc single cylinder two-stroke, maximum output 17.6 bhp (DIN) at 7,400 rpm. Bore and stroke 62×54 mm. Compression ratio 8.6:1. Bing carburettor. 50:1 petroil lubrication. Kick start.
Transmission: primary drive by gears; final by chain. Five-speed gearbox. Wet multiplate clutch.
Ignition: Bosch Thyristor contactless. 6v.
Frame: tubular duplex cradle.
Suspension: front, telescopic forks; rear, swinging arm.
Tyres: front, 2.75×18; rear, 3.25×18.
Brakes: front, 280 mm disc; rear, 160 mm drum.
Tank capacity: 3.2 gallons (14.2 litres).
Weight: 266 lbs (121 kg).
Maximum speed: approximately 74 mph (120 kmh).

Manufacturer: Zündapp-Werke GmbH, 8 München 80, Anzinger Strasse, 1-3.